On *Purpose*

Dedication

This book is dedicated to my wife, Suzanne, and our three girls: Kirby, Casey Elizabeth, and Lucy.

No better teachers did ever a man have.

SAMUEL CASEY CARTER

On *Purpose*

**How
Great School
Cultures
Form Strong
Character**

A Joint Publication

CORWIN
A SAGE Company

Center for Education Reform

For information:

Corwin
A SAGE Company
2455 Teller Road
Thousand Oaks,
    California 91320
(800) 233-9936
Fax: (800) 417-2466
www.corwin.com

SAGE India Pvt. Ltd.
B 1/I 1 Mohan Cooperative
    Industrial Area
Mathura Road, New Delhi 110 044
India

SAGE Ltd.
1 Oliver's Yard
55 City Road
London EC1Y 1SP
United Kingdom

SAGE Asia-Pacific Pte. Ltd.
33 Pekin Street #02-01
Far East Square
Singapore 048763

Printed in the United States of America

Library of Congress Cataloging-in-Publication Data

Carter, Samuel Casey.
On purpose : how great school cultures form strong character / Samuel Casey Carter.
    p. cm.
"A Joint Publication With The Center for Education Reform."
Includes bibliographical references and index.
ISBN 978-1-4129-8672-4 (pbk.)
    1. Moral education—United States—Case studies. 2. Character—Study and teaching—United States—Case studies. 3. Academic achievement—United States—Case studies. I. Center for Education Reform (Washington, D.C.) II. Title.

LC311.C277 2011
370.11'4--dc22   2010038712

This book is printed on acid-free paper.

10   11   12   13   14   10   9   8   7   6   5   4   3   2   1

Acquisitions Editor:	Arnis Burvikovs
Associate Editor:	Desirée Bartlett
Editorial Assistant:	Kimberly Greenberg
Production Editor:	Amy Schroller
Copy Editor:	Codi Bowman
Typesetter:	C&M Digitals (P) Ltd.
Proofreader:	Wendy Jo Dymond
Indexer:	Sylvia Coates
Cover Designer:	Rose Storey
Permissions Editor:	Karen Ehrmann

Contents

SECTION III: RESPONSE

Preface

Culture means a way of life of a group of people—the behaviors, beliefs, and truths they accept.

Character can mean one of two things: (1) that which someone really is—their nature as formed by habit or (2) the expression of a person's unique individuality.

S chools are made. This book is about how they are made well. By telling the stories of twelve very different but equally extraordinary schools from all across the country, this book explains how school cultures are made, how they form student character, and, ultimately, how great school cultures harness student character to drive achievement.

All schools have a culture. No school is without one. School culture shapes what occurs within the building and what happens without—whether for good or for ill. The key questions are simply what are the particular sources of your school's culture and what effect does it have on your school's outcomes.

Answering these questions well and having the means to harness school culture to drive positive outcomes, I believe, is *the* school leadership question of the next ten years.

Given the rate of change in our society at large and the speed with which recent high school and college graduates are expected to compete with their peers *worldwide* for the same jobs and opportunities, it has become the essential duty of all school leaders to create environments that overwhelmingly give students both the academic skills and the personal where-withal to compete successfully in a global economy.

This book profiles twelve outstanding schools that together provide a roadmap for anyone wishing to create a great school culture. In the detail of what these schools do and through the study of how they do it, the reader of this book will learn in practical terms how great school cultures are made and what is required to harness the transformational power of school culture to drive outstanding student outcomes.

FROM GOOD TO GREAT

The twelve extraordinary schools profiled later in these pages demonstrate that a school's faculty and administration, given the right priorities and a proper coordination of effort, can purposefully create a school culture that dramatically improves the lives of the children entrusted to their care. Further, these schools show that children who benefit from these environments experience a renewed sense of self and an individual sense of purpose that can then be tapped to drive remarkable student achievement.

Although it may be surprising that a particular school culture would produce equally good athletes, good citizens, good artists, and good scholars, it turns out to be very common that a schoolwide focus on what it means to be good—a culture of character—is at the root of many schools being great.

In its simplest formulation, the schools highlighted here teach us that if children are taught to be good, they can learn to be great. The level of accomplishment regularly achieved in these schools is astounding, but it would not be possible without the moral excellence that precedes it. Seriousness and hard work are required to do well in school, but for the faculty and administrations of the schools profiled here, it is their schoolwide attention to *student happiness* first that makes this level of achievement possible.

What happens to students in these schools happens *on purpose*. And so these schools are celebrated for the remarkable degree to which they purposefully shape their school cultures to achieve very certain outcomes. But there is more here.

No matter how well *intentioned* our school systems may be, the absolute priority in schools today is not placed first on the individual well-being—let alone on the *intended* happiness—of each individual student. The schools profiled here quite simply teach that schools are for children; structured in any other way, they lose their *purpose*. These schools also teach us that to be effective, school cultures have to be *intentional*. School cultures have to be purposefully constructed to produce very particular outcomes. If they are not intentional, if they are not explicit about what they want to achieve and how they intend to achieve it, then they invite every form of mixed message to dilute their overall mission or diminish their ability to execute on it.

And that's the point. The risk of not purposefully focusing on school culture is that you risk inviting every possible alternative to what you ultimately want for your school.

Although this single observation should be sufficient to get schools and communities focused on creating great school cultures that form strong character, there are three reasons why this topic that is so important to the success of our children gets lost among other discussions.

THREE FALSE STARTS

First, the academic and popular literature on schooling has almost a cultlike fascination with the role of school leadership in driving great outcomes. To the detriment of our understanding about school climate and culture, we have focused almost exclusively on leadership. However important the role of the school principal may be, we must not forget that the primary job of all senior leaders is to create the proper *work environment* and then effectively *motivate* those who work there. Too much of the discussion surrounding school principals has failed to recognize the many elements outside of school leadership that shape a school environment, let alone how the workers in that environment are best motivated. Most especially, this discussion surrounding school principals has failed to notice that in every school in the world, the greatest amount of work is done—or should be done—by *students,* and so it is *they* who most need to be motivated by the environment.

Second, school culture is often presented as a topic of such complexity that it cannot possibly be managed to yield certain outcomes. This is simply untrue. "School-Level Factors," as Robert Marzano (2003) and others have rightly identified them, are a well-understood subset of the total number of influences on student outcomes. School-level factors, however, drive teacher-level effects, and in the end, it is overall teacher quality that is the single most accurate indicator of a student's performance in school (Sanders & Rivers, 1996). If school cultures do not create environments in which teachers are intrinsically rewarded for their hard work and so willingly contribute their very best efforts, then the school will miss the mark. This book aims to fix this mistake.

Third, but perhaps most importantly, the discussion of school culture as it is presented here is intended as an antidote to so much discussion of character education as it is popularly understood. However well intended, what passes for character education is often so hopelessly thin and so irregularly supported that it has little lasting effect on the moral formation of students and even less impact on the broader activities they engage in across any given school day. Although some of these shortcomings can be overcome through better program design, it is the strong opinion of many people featured in this book that character education programs often unintentionally (and unknowingly) undermine their stated purpose. In this book, we argue that to work at all such programs must first be entirely reoriented to a greater good. By making the low goals of "disciplined behavior" or "caring kids" their main objective, these efforts typically miss altogether the fundamental truth that human happiness is the greatest catalyst of human excellence. In stark contrast to so much "character education programming," the schools featured here demonstrate that when schools are properly ordered, they naturally become centers of both happiness and excellence.

Consistent with this way of thinking, the schools profiled in this book demonstrate a very simple but profound truth: Schools become great by creating a culture in which confident children joyfully strive to accomplish worthy goals in concert with their friends. What is more, the children in these schools understand why this striving is good and what this requires of them and their fellow students. On the other hand, too many efforts at character education just aim for a more mild-mannered school. In so doing they tear at the heart and soul of what makes real teaching and learning such a passionate exercise.

Taken altogether, the schools profiled here remind us what great schooling looks like and what concrete steps we can take to create many more great schools like them.

Acknowledgments

First and foremost, I want to thank the entire staff of the Center for Education Reform for supporting the research behind this book and for sponsoring my work as a senior fellow over the last three years. Special thanks go to Jeanne Allen, Matthew Ballard, Tim Barley, Alison Consoletti, Taylor Curilla, Cheryl Hillen, Dawn Jenets, Kara Hornung Kerwin, Dora Kingsley, Anita Korten, David Monge, Jonathan Oglesby, and Maiya Turnage. In the initial stages of this project, I benefited most especially from the research assistance of John Allen, Dan Willerth, Kevin Gibson, Leslie Rutledge, and Sammi Strickland Hawkins.

The research for this effort was entirely funded by the Kern Family Foundation and the John Templeton Foundation. Without the original commitment of Ryan Olson, who was the first to sign on to this project, and the enthusiasm of Kimon Sargeant, who was the first to appreciate its potential, this book never would have been written.

To the parents, teachers, administrators, but most especially the students of all the schools I visited while writing this book—both those profiled here and the many that were not included   your words run throughout these pages.

And to Kirby, Casey, and Lucy, but most of all, my wife Suzanne, who continues to be the surest inspiration for the very best of my efforts, it is to the four of you that this book and all my work is dedicated.

Publisher's Acknowledgments

Corwin gratefully acknowledges the contributions and editorial insights from the following individuals:

Mary Beth Klee, Author of *Core Virtues*

Irwin Kurz, Director of School Quality
National Heritage Academies
Brooklyn, NY

Steven Miletto, EdD, Principal
R. L. Osborne High School
Marietta, GA

William H. Wibel
SchoolWorks, LLC
Beverly, MA

About the Author

 **Samuel Casey Carter** wrote this book as senior fellow at the Center for Education Reform, an advocacy organization based in Washington, D.C., whose mission is to change laws, minds, and cultures so that good schools might flourish. Today he is president of CfBT USA, the United States charity affiliated with CfBT Education Trust headquartered in the United Kingdom. Previously, Carter was president of National Heritage Academies, a charter school management company that operates more than sixty public charter schools in six states, where he oversaw corporate strategy and the implementation of the company's educational operations.

Carter is also the author of *No Excuses: Lessons From 21 High-Performing, High-Poverty Schools*, a book on the effective practices of high-performing schools that refuse to make poverty an excuse for academic failure. In addition to *No Excuses*, Carter has edited three other books including Mary Beth Klee's *Core Virtues*, a literature-based character education program for parents and teachers of elementary school students. His articles, essays, and columns have appeared in more than 180 newspapers and magazines, including

The Wall Street Journal, Chicago Tribune, The New York Times, New York Post, The Washington Times, Los Angeles Times, Investor's Business Daily, and *The Detroit News.*

After receiving a bachelor degree from St. John's College in Annapolis in philosophy and mathematics, Carter studied theology at Oxford University and philosophy at the Catholic University of America. He lives in Washington, D.C., with his wife Suzanne, whom he met while they were both teachers, and their three girls: Kirby, Casey Elizabeth, and Lucy.

SECTION I
Theory

1

Four Common Traits of Great School Cultures

This book was written while I served as a senior fellow at the Center for Education Reform (CER) in Washington, D.C. CER is an advocacy organization whose mission is to change laws, minds, and cultures so that good schools might flourish.

For more than fifteen years, CER has amassed one of the largest national repositories of primary and secondary literature on school performance. It was with access to these resources that the research team at CER and I examined close to 3,500 schools over the course of a year looking for mainstream-American schools that have not been widely promoted as examples of great school culture but whose cultures demonstrate an extraordinary commitment to strong character development and the teaching of the whole child.

From this initial pass, we identified nearly 350 high-performing schools with a reputation for instilling strong personal character. The goal in the end was to arrive at a set of geographically, demographically and programmatically diverse schools that together could tell a larger story about how school cultures are formed and how they can be shaped in a very certain way to have the most positive effect on student outcomes.

HOW AND WHY THESE SCHOOLS WERE SELECTED

To arrive at the set of schools profiled here, we first removed schools that in our estimate pursue a more "programmatic" approach to character development—as opposed to developing a comprehensive school culture committed to strong character. Next, we removed many of the most storied schools in the country that have extraordinary school cultures that readers might dismiss as being "unscalable" or inapplicable to their circumstances—especially elite private schools and strict observance religious schools. At this stage, we also eliminated schools that some would identify as too "autocratic," for example, military academies and reform schools, preferring instead to tell the story of schools where the moral order comes more from inside and is more explicitly voluntarily chosen.

From these, the team prepared a comparative study of thirty-nine schools in preparation for in-person school visits and interviews with the parents, students, faculty, and administrative leaders at each school. After my field visits were complete, I decided to profile the twelve schools featured here.

Altogether, they come from nine states in the north, south, east, west, and midwestern regions of the country. Ten of the twelve are public schools—two of these public schools are charters, three are magnets, and two of these magnets have a preferential option for the economically disadvantaged. The two private schools are both of religious orientation. These characteristics are summarized in Figure 1.1.

Figure 1.1 Featured Schools

Name of School	Type	Students	Grades
Arlington Traditional, Arlington, VA	Public Magnet	442	PK–5
P.S. 124, New York, NY	Local Public	1143	PK–8
An Achievable Dream, Newport News, VA	Public Magnet	987	PK–12
Cotswold Elementary, Charlotte, NC	Public Magnet	499	K–5
Grayhawk Elementary, Scottsdale, AZ	Local Public	821	K–6
Atlantis Elementary, Port St. John, FL	Local Public	720	K–6
Benjamin Franklin, Franklin, MA	Public Charter	394	K–6
Hope Prima, Milwaukee, WI	Private	220	K–8
Providence St. Mel, Chicago, IL	Private	650	K–12
Harvest Park Middle School, Pleasanton, CA	Local Public	1129	6–8
Veritas Academy, Phoenix, AZ	Public Charter	322	6–12
Hinsdale Central H.S., Hinsdale, IL	Local Public	2624	9–12

Together, they serve the broadest range of diversity that is seen in American schooling: Four serve minority low-income students, three serve lower-middle to middle-income families, four serve middle- to upper-middle-income families, and one is almost a statistically perfect mix of minority, white, low-, middle-, upper-middle-, and upper-income children. Two are preK or kindergarten to fifth grade. Three are kindergarten to sixth grade. Two are preK or kindergarten to eighth grade. One is a middle school (6–8), one is a middle-high school (6–12), one is a high school (9–12), and two are preK or kindergarten to twelfth grade. The demographics of these schools are summarized in Figure 1.2.

Figure 1.2 Demographics of the Featured Schools

Name of School	Ethnicity					Median Income
	White	Hispanic	Black	Asian	Other	
Arlington Traditional, Arlington, VA	59	12	8	21	0	Medium
P.S. 124, New York, NY	3	21	36	40	0	Low
An Achievable Dream, Newport News, VA	1	2	96	0	0	Low
Cotswold Elementary, Charlotte, NC	45	11	43	0	0	Medium
Grayhawk Elementary, Scottsdale, AZ	88	3	2	7	0	Medium High
Atlantis Elementary, Port St. John, FL	81	5	6	0	7	Medium
Benjamin Franklin, Franklin, MA	89	1	1	8	0	Medium
Hope Prima, Milwaukee, WI	0	1	99	0	0	Low
Providence St. Mel, Chicago, IL	0	1	99	0	0	Low
Harvest Park Middle School, Pleasanton, CA	59	0	3	26	2	Medium High
Veritas Academy, Phoenix, AZ	91	5	1	0	3	Medium
Hinsdale Central H.S., Hinsdale, IL	81	4	3	12	0	High

All of these schools beat the competition in their local areas as far as academic and other student achievement is concerned. All of them far exceed the national performance levels for the populations they serve. Nine of the twelve would rank superior on any national ranking of any kind. Together, they are just a snapshot of the more than 115,000 schools in the country, but they are among the very best—for they aim only to bring the best out of their students—and they prove what is possible for every school in America.

FOUR COMMON TRAITS

The great value in the study of these schools is not in any general framework, but in the details. The beauty of these schools is in what they do and how they do it, so to understand them correctly, we have to address each of them on their own terms.

This is, after all, exactly what these schools teach us about children: If we do not address *who* they are first, we cannot hope to learn *what* they can do. For this reason, the great bulk of this book is dedicated to twelve school profiles that highlight some of the novel features of each school and focus on particular aspects or practices at the heart of that school's extraordinary school culture.

That said, these twelve schools and these twelve very particular profiles of them also tell a larger story about how school cultures are made, how school cultures form character, and how great school cultures harness character to drive achievement. To help the reader apply these lessons to their circumstances, the next chapter addresses each of these themes in brief. But first, a quick overview of what these schools have in common.

There are literally dozens of ways to organize the many common elements shared by the schools profiled in these pages. Their school cultures are often founded on similar or related principles, they regularly have like effects on their surrounding communities, and of course, they share many of the same practices. But in the words of the students, teachers, and

administrators who work in the great school cultures celebrated here, it is the following four traits that provide the most
insight into what they have in common:

1. A strong belief that culture determines outcomes

2. A nurturing but demanding culture

3. A culture committed to student success

4. A culture of people, principles, and purpose

These four traits, however, do not surface one after the other to
form a school culture—they are not steps or the means to a great
school. Further, it is unclear whether these four traits emerge in dif-
fering degrees to shape schools of various quality. Whether these
four traits are on display to some degree in lower-performing
schools, I cannot say. But in great school cultures that form strong
personal character, it is absolutely certain that they are all four in
evidence—like a formula or a necessary pattern that once in place
provides the occasion for all the benefits that follow.

1. A Strong Belief That Culture Determines Outcomes

All schools have an identity that affects the identity of the
children in them. There is no other way to say this. In addition
to what is explicitly taught, there is a great deal that is implicitly learned throughout the school day, and great school cultures work hard to make sure these teachings are consistent
with what they value most. The immense amount of work
required to intentionally shape a school culture has its origins
in the strong belief that culture determines outcomes and that
the work is worth it.

If you do not believe in the transformational influence that
school culture has on everything and everyone in your school,
then much that takes place around you will occur well outside
your control because it will not be done *on purpose.*

Schools that most powerfully wish to shape their student outcomes through their school culture, therefore, take concrete steps to establish clear, outward expressions of this inward belief. It is only in knowing exactly what you *intend* for your school to achieve that you can begin to do it each and every day *on purpose.*

2. A NURTURING BUT DEMANDING CULTURE

How great school cultures make rigorous and regular demands on everyone associated with them without overplaying their hand or overstaying their welcome is perhaps the single most important quality to look for and understand in the school profiles that follow. They aim to achieve a perfect balance between a nurturing and demanding culture by *nurturing the person first* while looking for every opportunity to stretch the skills, attainments, and natural attributes of all their community members—parents, students, and teachers alike.[1]

Excellence for these schools always means being the very best *you* can be. The goal is not a perfection of excellence but a *striving* to do *your* best, which means great school cultures begin nurturing the true character of each individual first.

Although each of these schools achieves this balance in various ways and through various devices, they do not attempt to plant the seed without first tilling the soil. A clear common trait across all of these schools is that they focus on establishing *authentic relationships* between students and their teachers before they expect those teachers to be able to make authentic and worthy demands of their students.

3. A CULTURE COMMITTED TO STUDENT SUCCESS

The students in the schools celebrated here possess a number of remarkable qualities with astonishing regularity. They are effective communicators, enthusiastic learners, and emerging leaders. As we will see in a moment, they are confident team players who learn to take intelligent risks. But above all else, they are joyful, cheerful, and happy. This is how they are described by their teachers, by their families, and by themselves.

Students in great school cultures understand the adults in their lives want them to succeed. It is precisely because so many influential adults assume their success and are demonstrably committed to their individual achievement that the students in these schools learn to accept the sacrifices of hard work and learn to desire the great good that can come of it. But it is equally important that students are given *specific means to succeed,* so in the schools profiled here, students are given specific tools to help them *do* the things that are expected of them.

Schools are for children. Classrooms must be student centered. This is not a learned educational philosophy but a simple truth. For students to learn well, teachers must teach well, which means they must be passionate about great teaching and committed to continually learning how best to connect with each of their students through the subject matter in question and through the particular needs of each child. Above all else, this is what it means for a school culture to be committed to student success.

4. A CULTURE OF PEOPLE, PRINCIPLES, AND PURPOSE

The schools profiled here are celebrated for doing their work *on purpose* as opposed to so many others that are not so intentional in their action, principled in their outlook, or purpose driven from the start. For each of these schools, it takes extraordinary people—with actions that are directed by clear principles—to create a school culture that knows what it is doing and achieves its goals on purpose.

But let us not understate what we mean. School cultures do not become great simply by doing what they set out to do. Rather, greatness comes when they invite the opportunity for greatness in others, when they demand principled action and genuinely encourage their students to pursue *life's purpose*. Today, this means that schools once again need to become places that teach about the true, the good, and the beautiful, and to do so, they must create an environment in which the true, the good, and the beautiful can be experienced firsthand.

To understand these four common traits more fully, let us turn now to consider how great school cultures are created.

2

Creating a Great School Culture

This chapter covers three topics: (1) how school cultures are made, (2) how school cultures form character, and (3) how great school cultures harness character to drive achievement. Let's take each of these themes in turn.

How School Cultures Are Made

Great school cultures take shape in four stages:

1. School culture begins to form in response to a need.

2. School culture commits to certain founding principles.

3. School culture begins to shape outcomes.

4. Customs and habits are further embedded to improve outcomes.

As Figure 2.1 tries to depict, school culture begins with a clear sense of mission or need to which the school culture itself will become the response. At this early stage, relatively few people (perhaps only the founders, a few administrators, or a handful of teachers) may be involved, but as the school culture takes root and begins to grow, the number of people involved in shaping the school culture soon involves the entire school community.

Figure 2.1

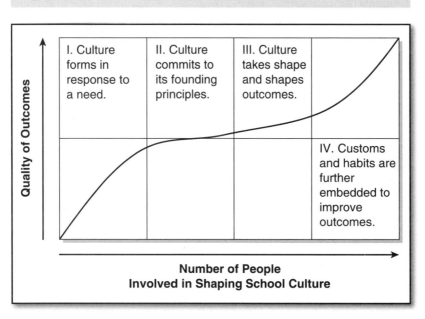

As the Figure 2.1 also tries to depict, the quality of outcomes produced by an emerging school culture is directly related to the number of people involved in shaping that school culture. As this number of people grows—and the extent to which customs and habits created by the culture are further embedded within it—the quality of these outcomes only improves further. Let us look at each of these four stages in the context of the school profiles that will follow shortly.

1. School Culture Begins to Form in Response to a Need

In the first stage, the school culture begins to emerge as a response to a certain need. The schools profiled in this book have been started from scratch, and they have been re-created after decades of being something else. They have slowly matured over time or quickly assumed their tremendous qualities. But in every instance, these schools are a response— they represent a deliberate choice to do things differently— and the school culture becomes an outward expression of what they believe and why they believe it.

Hinsdale Central High School set out to reculture its school after a terrible tragedy, P.S. 124 sought more academic rigor for their students, Arlington Traditional School needed a student–teacher relationship that was more engaging than what was being offered in the open-classroom of the 1970s, and An Achievable Dream and HOPE Prima needed to create child-centered havens away from the low expectations of the street. But all of these schools begin as a challenge to the *status quo*, wanting something more for the students they serve.

2. School Culture Commits to Certain Founding Principles

Every school has the ability to monitor and manage its message—so that a child is not hearing three or four competing messages in a given day—but it requires tremendous focus and a coordinated effort. In this second stage, the schools profiled here commit themselves to what they believe and put down on paper what principles drive their shared purpose.

Grayhawk outlined the "Other 3Rs"; Arlington Traditional School has the "ABCs of Success"; Benjamin Franklin relies on the virtues of "Prudence, Temperance, Fortitude, and Justice"; and Harvest Park committed to "Compassion, Honesty, Respect, Responsibility, Integrity, and Self-Discipline." Above all else, these great school cultures state what virtues or habits of character they expect to see on display at all times from the members of their community.

3. Culture Begins to Shape Outcomes

If culture is a way of life of a group of people—the behaviors, beliefs, and truths they accept—then it is in this third stage that the school culture really begins to take shape and shape new outcomes. Several critical things happen at once: Slogans, rites, rituals, and other traditions that embody the school's principles begin to emerge while more people of like mind are drawn to the school's purpose and its commitment to principle.

It is most often at this stage that a school culture becomes known for its welcoming environment and recognized for its positive effects, not only on the students and teachers but also on the community more broadly.

4. Customs and Habits Are Further Embedded to Improve Outcomes

This fourth stage is regularly experienced as a virtuous cycle. Now that the culture has successfully institutionalized what it values, it is able to spread its message more consistently over a larger number of constituents and draw on greater resources to further the development of its culture.

Now that the school has experienced firsthand the benefits of its principled approach, it commits itself further to these principles and finds richer, more innovative, and longer lasting means to express what it holds most dear. The number of people and resources committed to the culture also increases—often increasing the positive effects proportionately. The overall climate of the school, for example, might move from safe and orderly to genuinely cheerful and high achieving.

During this same stage, or at any time earlier, schools can also fall away from their adherence to their principled approach and watch their school culture decline in the process.

How School Cultures Form Character

What positive character formation means, sadly, has often been confused with effective behavior management. If students are well behaved, schools are often satisfied with that. For schools of that kind, if they have a character program of some kind in place, disciplined students are a sign—to them—that their character education works. Alternatively, if schools have well-mannered and well-behaved children, these schools often fail to ask how student character is being formed. What may be worse, if they have ill-behaved students, the concern is not first for their character but how can these students most easily be brought into line?

This is not the case with school cultures that aim to form strong personal character. As Father Dick Rieman, chaplain to the girls at the Montrose School in Medfield, Massachusetts, has memorably said, "Good friends help you make good choices." Great school cultures aim to bring young people together in an environment that teaches them what a good friend is, helps them qualify what makes for a good choice, and, ultimately, teaches them to work together both for their individual and collective good.

Although there is quite a lot here to process, the genius of the schools profiled in this book is they make it easier to take in. The power in creating an intentionally formed culture is that everything in the school is aligned with what matters most. When everyone in the community understands that their personal character is at the heart of the school's success, the school as a whole can work together to bring everyone along. This is how great school cultures work.

Without exception, the key to getting this right, according to the parents, faculty, students, and administration of all twelve schools profiled here, is that the school culture must make this explicit. If it is valued, then it must be publicly stated—early and often. This is the role of vision statements, mission statements, student creeds, pledges, placards, and posters that remind the community why character is critical to its success.[2]

Similarly, if all *routines* must be character building, every *location* must present an opportunity to express one's good character.

All places in the school, but especially common areas, must have an explicit purpose, and the purpose of that place must be honored through consistently enforced expectations. The easiest place for a culture of character to be compromised is any one of the informal meeting areas, where relaxing what we do, we might relax what we stand for. To address this, school communities have to figure out what are the virtues that can be learned and practiced in each of the locations throughout the school. The great school cultures celebrated here do not, as a result, become puritanical or prudish; they become intentional, and more than anything, they intend on forming personal character well.

How Great School Cultures Drive Achievement

People do well what they do often—and we are inspired to do more often what we enjoy doing. This is not simply about pleasure and pain or reward and punishment; rather, this is about learning what is truly good, learning to desire it more intensely, and working harder to obtain it.

Students in great school cultures enjoy the hard work, and they do not find it unmanageable. Their commitment to hard work leads to real achievement, which leads to further joy—both in what they have learned and what they have accomplished. As was said in the Preface, "Seriousness and hard work are required to do well in school, but for the faculty and administrations of the schools profiled here, it is their schoolwide attention to student happiness first that makes this level of achievement possible." What this means can now be explained more fully.

Great school cultures are founded on principles to which the entire school community is committed. Great school cultures are explicit about what is valued, about what is truly good, and about what they aim for. Through intentional practices and purposeful activity, they help the entire community strive in this direction. But let us not forget, at the beginning of all this striving, there is first a commitment to the individual character formation of each person in the school community.

It is through the school's commitment to principle that the community learns *what* is good, but it is through the school's commitment to the character formation of each individual person in that community that each person learns for him- or herself that *he* or *she* is good. This is transformational.

Three things happen to school cultures because of this transformation that, in turn, makes them great. First, this clear understanding of what the community values and that each person is intrinsically valued by the community manifests itself in extraordinary personal *confidence*. More than any other quality, the schools featured here are recognizable for the joyful, cheerful, happy disposition of their students that comes from knowing who they are and how they fit in. Similarly, faculty members are satisfied in their jobs, and they say it is the intrinsic reward of the job that keeps them there.

Second, it is because great school cultures so successfully nurture the personal confidence and individual character of each person in the community that those characters become even more potent as *team players* committed to a common cause. Citizens of great school cultures work well together, they work hard together, and they work hard to do well because they want the same things for themselves and for the community as a whole.

Third, it is because great school cultures so successfully create a team spirit committed to achieving the same goals that they also inspire intelligent *risk-taking* toward the further achievement of what the community values most. People who feel loved—and valued for who they are—feel free to fail in the achievement of difficult things. People who honestly feel a part of a family—and a community that is both greater than them and unwilling to let them down—feel free to reach higher, confident that what they are doing is good, and that someone is there to catch them if they fall.

As we will see in the following pages, it is through this simple three-step process that great school cultures harness strong personal character to drive extraordinary achievement.

SECTION II
Practice

3

Harvest Park Middle School

Pleasanton, California

School Information	
4900 Valley Avenue Pleasanton, CA 94566 Phone: (925) 425–4444 Fax: (925) 426–9613	Public 1,129 students Grades 6 through 8 59% white, 26% Asian, 3% Filipino, 2% black

Cultural Traits Highlighted	Key Practices Featured

• A strong belief that culture determines outcomes	• Six expected behaviors:
	  (1) compassion
	  (2) honesty
	  (3) respect
	  (4) responsibility
	  (5) integrity
	  (6) self-discipline
	• Broadcast of *Daily Bulletin*

• A culture committed to student success	• Common language across the school • Authentic opportunities to lead • Sense of family among students and faculty
• A culture of people, principles, and purpose	• Patriot Path

By any standard, Harvest Park is an extraordinary school. Across a breadth of academic and extracurricular offerings rare even among elite private institutions, this local public middle school has established a record of student achievement that is more enviable still. If you concentrate too carefully, however, on the many details that distance Harvest Park from a more typical public school experience (the award-winning robotics club, the jazz ensemble, the string orchestra, the student-run television studio, and so on), you just may miss what makes Harvest Park so special. However simple it may sound, the school culture at Harvest Park is one created by a common language, clear expectations, and a faculty and student body who care for one another more like a family.

COMMON LANGUAGE

Harvest Park is one of four middle schools among seventeen schools total that together form the Pleasanton Unified School District. Pleasanton is a suburban town some thirty miles southeast of Oakland, California. Although the village may be fairly described as slightly old-fashioned—with antique wooden signs and storefronts that have not changed much in the last fifty years—the composition of the town itself is very much a picture of present-day Middle America, even if it is home to some important cultural icons like the NFL's John Madden and *Dilbert's* cartoon creator Scott Adams. As of the 2000 census, Pleasanton was a town of 63,600 souls—80% of whom were white, nearly 12% Asian, with the remaining 8% Hispanic or Latino (MDNH, 2010). Overall, the socioeconomics can be fairly described as upper-middle income.

As its name suggests, however, Pleasanton is a special place. Since 1996 when a citywide initiative to create a "community of character" was implemented, the community, as a whole, has worked together to create an atmosphere and model behaviors that instill personal, social, and civic responsibility. The goal for the community is to build good habits of action and foster the reflection required to help all its citizens internalize a number of expected behaviors. Through a communitywide survey, six expected behaviors were identified: (1) compassion, (2) honesty, (3) respect, (4) responsibility, (5) integrity, and (6) self-discipline. Today, when you drive through Pleasanton, you'll see signs and banners posted in key locations that in bold letters promote a different one of these virtues each month, **INTEGRITY**, for example, and then a sign that reminds you, "Pleasanton: a community of character." Even with these expected behaviors in hand, the question at the school district level was how best to support teachers in their broader effort to instill character in their students? Inspired by early efforts at Lydiksen Elementary, Harvest Park soon proved what was possible.

The Town of Pleasanton: A Community of Character

After trying a number of the commercially available programs, Harvest Park decided to take a more comprehensive approach. "As a staff, we decided all canned character programs were add-ons that would never add up to much," explains Jim Hansen, who has been the principal at Harvest Park since this initiative was announced. "We needed a platform that wasn't extra. More than anything else, we needed a way of *talking* to the students."

Like many school leaders, of the quieter type, who shape their school culture by empowering others and giving them the direction and support they need to be successful, Hansen chooses his words very deliberately, but they emerge with a clarity that comes from a sure sense of purpose. "We're all about giving the children words and phrases they need to be more effective. Especially in matters of right and wrong, children want to do the right thing, but they often don't have the words to do it."

As a simple example, students at Harvest Park are encouraged to say, "Can you use another word, please?" if ever they don't like what someone is saying (using foul language) or how they might be saying it (to bully or intimidate another student). Even if the phrase may sound slightly precious at first, it becomes extraordinarily powerful in the voice of a child once it is used in common across an entire student body, and everyone knows to hold themselves in check when they hear it.

Even more common, since the practice has been in place much longer, you'll hear students say, "Don't be a shark," or you'll notice signs posted in the hallways (both in English and Spanish) that read "shark-free zone." Being a shark refers to any kind of bullying or unacceptable behavior. Middle school students, almost by nature it seems, can be very cruel—and often without knowing what they are doing. By giving the children the words they need to distinguish right from wrong, and the encouragement to label as wrong any behavior that cannot be condoned, every child at Harvest Park becomes a part of the solution and an additional means by which its culture of character is more effectively transmitted.

The sum total of all that is expected of students at Harvest Park is called the "Patriot Path," which emphasizes both the school's mascot of the Patriot and the school's larger belief that what students learn at Harvest Park is essential for them to assume their responsibilities in a democratic society. Even more essential, Hansen notes, "You are either on the path or off it," once again demonstrating his penchant for communicating expectations both simply and unequivocally. A great deal is required to remain on the Patriot Path. A high standard of academic, athletic, artistic, and other activities is expected of all students at Harvest Park, but the level of support and community encouragement provided is also extraordinary (as evidenced by the well-executed school handbooks, student orientation, parent orientation, student ambassadors, mentors, advisers, and so many other school assets). Taken all together, it provides an important lesson in the range of coordinated effort required to keep the whole community on the Patriot Path and the school culture as a whole headed in the right direction.

Every morning students who have been trained through the school's highly selective media class are responsible for a live broadcast of the school's *Daily Bulletin,* which is carried in every classroom on Channel 86 via the school's closed-circuit TV network. The students are responsible for all technical aspects of the program as well as a good deal of the content. Every day the program is designed to include a reflection on the virtue of the month that aligns with Pleasanton's community of character campaign, further unifying the school culture around this language and the behavioral expectations it sets for the entire community.

"Closed-circuit TV is great device, but it is just a device," Hansen observes. "What is essential is an effective means of communicating with the children."

On this particular day, Randy Lomas, one the school's more beloved math teachers, is reading an extended reflection on integrity while another teacher, Jana Halle, who oversees the media program, is playing the role of character EDwina, a muppet, looking over Mr. Lomas's shoulder:

TV Studio Broadcast of the *Daily Bulletin* Run Entirely by Students

Spencer Johnson explains it this way, "Integrity is telling myself the truth. And honesty is telling the truth to other people." That's a good start; let's see what else we can do with it. . . . Integrity is your character—it's the real you. Your integrity determines how you'll act in difficult situations—how you'll act if you're tempted to do that which you know to be wrong. Integrity is something we expect from those we look up to—a character trait we recognize and admire when we see it. To become the person you really want to be, you must demand it of yourself.

While Mr. Lomas continues his reflection, students in the television studio adjust some volume controls and change an adjoining set in anticipation of the upcoming sports announcements. Meanwhile, the students in the classroom immediately adjacent, visible through the glass of the television studio, listen attentively to Mr. Lomas's message, some with their eyes on the classroom's television monitor and others with their eyes closed or looking down at their desks. The respectful attitude of quiet concentration is unmistakable. When Mr. Lomas concludes and character EDwina waves good-bye, the *Daily Bulletin* cuts quickly to a series of announcements to brief everyone on the details of the day ahead. Mr. Hansen jumps in during one spot, but the whole affair appears to move quite smoothly with very little adult presence in evidence. One student anchorman reminds the eighth graders that even though it is crazy-hat day for spirit week, there will be no hats worn during the eighth-grade class portrait taken later that morning. A few students nod their heads in the class next door—a good, if obvious, reminder. Staying on the Patriot Path takes vigilance and some serious attention to detail.

CLEAR EXPECTATIONS

"School is an environment that is *controlled*. If children don't thrive in school, they have little chance of surviving in a more demanding environment," Randy Lomas remarks during a preparation period that the teachers use to plan lessons and collaborate with one another to improve their instruction. "The point is, in order for a school environment and school culture to be *good*, it has to be genuinely and properly *controlled*." This is an observation that requires some level of interpretation coming as it does from a man whose classroom is, at times, a study in creative chaos.

Randy Lomas sits with his desk off to the side, stationed as if to get out of the way, while twenty-eight eighth graders in an honors geometry class try to solve for x as quickly as they can. Mr. Lomas writes out an equation projected from his tablet computer to a screen at the front of the room:

$$\sin x = 7/25$$

"Everybody know *how* to do it?" Lomas asks. "Quickly now. Who's got the answer?" At least fourteen hands go up.

Several others go up an instant later, but a couple of those students are also clearly still drawing out the right triangle projected on the screen and labeling its sides just as quickly to make sure they have the right trigonometric ratio.

"Who wants a calculator? Everybody gets a calculator. Quick. Get the calculators," Lomas barks excitedly, like some friendly dog at a local park glad that so many others are happy to play with him. Nearly a dozen children race across the classroom to get scientific calculators for them and their fellow classmates. "Quickly now!" Lomas keeps writing on his tablet computer and more figures appear on the screen.

In the midst of this frenzy, you notice the room is literally wallpapered in certificates, trophies, and other booty won at state and national mathematics contests over the years. As the students with the calculators race back to their desks, we learn the value of x, and the class cheers in unison and pre-pares to do three other related problems now written out for all to see. Looking up—smiling—and adjusting in his chair slightly to face the screen at front, Mr. Lomas looks fondly upon his students as they work. Behind him, you see there is a T-shirt stapled to the wall that says "Math never spells fun." Hardly.

"It matters not what they *learn* here," Lomas continues from the private conversation earlier. "What matters is who they *become*. And it's our job to help them do that well." Without hes-itation, he then applies the moral importance of his job to the practical skills he conveys in his math class each day: "Great problem solvers know how to solve problems they don't know how to solve at first." Lomas concludes by saying, "That's really what teachers do in a great school culture: They help children learn how to live a life that has not yet been lived." While learning this larger lesson, it turns out that they learn a great deal of math as well. Of the 431 eighth-grade students in last year's class, only *four* of them did not complete at least one year of algebra. More than fifty eighth-grade students from Harvest Park will enter high school this fall having already completed a full year of algebra and a full year of geometry. Still others are in Algebra 2, Precalculus, or have already completed Advance-Placement Calculus.

Jana Halle also teaches math. "Consequences are real here. Children need boundaries. Children need clear definition of what is right and what is wrong," Halle remarks directly but in a fashion that not only lacks all sternness but also somehow carries a warmth about it making it more attractive.

"Life is better when you are held accountable," Halle says, smiling in conclusion. "Children have to learn to get comfortable with that. That's what children at this age really need to learn." It quickly becomes apparent that Harvest Park is a place where children are given a lot of responsibility and a lot of authentic opportunities to lead, along with the very clear expectation that they can and will succeed if they continue to strive and continue to do their very best in everything they do. "They learn what they want to be defined by," Lomas adds to Halle's observations. "They play football, and they're really good at it, perhaps, but they know they don't want to be *defined* as a football player."

These strong relationships, in and out of the classroom, lead to a lot of hard work. A discussion with students between classes makes this clear. "If we act like children, we get treated like children," a seventh grader says. "But mostly the teachers push us to push ourselves more. Not by making it scary, but by making it fun to do more."

This notion of striving is clearly at the heart of the Patriot Path, but it is remarkable how often students and teachers alike stress that the hard work at Harvest Park is only made possible by a school culture that looks out for the deeper needs and personal identity of each and every child in it. "If children aren't grounded, you can't push them forward," notes Paul Robeck, a teacher for fifteen years at Harvest Park. "You can't build a child up—either academically or emotionally—unless they have a clear sense of self to build upon. You want to push, you want to show them they can always do more, but you can't just *push on*." Robeck leans forward to emphasize the absolute certainty of this next insight. "If you don't take the time to learn who they *are,* you'll have a very hard time achieving *depth* in your subject."

Lynn Gatehouse, who runs the school's robotics class, puts it this way: "Genuine personal connections enable teachers to draw out students through their other interests. Oftentimes, that's how children ultimately learn whatever subject matter you wanted to teach them in the first place." Gatehouse knows of what she speaks and not just because more than 120 students are actively engaged in robotics—giving her a full-time career in making connections through alternative means. Gatehouse also sent two of her children through Harvest Park, and she speaks openly about how the entire faculty rallied around her when she was diagnosed with a brain tumor a few years back. "Our family had the Harvest Park community. My children didn't miss a beat." Harvest Park teaches that it takes real human connections like these to make for real student progress—both in good times and in bad.

SCHOOL AND FAMILY

This theme of school as a family that enables children to learn who they really are and to take greater risks pursuing more difficult things because they are safe is an important one. It is important for the formation of both their moral and intellectual virtues it turns out. "Our school is a community. Our students see us around town, they know what we're interested in, and they know that we're interested in them," Jana Halle says, noting that she lives directly across the street from the school's main entrance. "A strong sense of community creates a real sense of openness. Problems don't get swept under the rug, but they are discussed and dealt with," Randy Lomas adds. A discussion with students makes this point even more concrete. "There is no bullying here. At other schools it isn't cool to work hard or to be smart. As a result, kids don't feel safe to be smart."

"What drives us here?" asks Marc Acheson. "It is a common vision that we want students of character who will make

Students in Harvest Park Courtyard

good choices in life both in and out of school. To do that, we all understand that we get their attention through topics that are of real interest to them." Despite what the students said about the absence of bullying, recently the faculty had to publicly address their concern over a rash of bullying episodes taking place both on and off campus. However mild these unwelcome deeds may have been, the act of bullying is so antithetical to the culture at Harvest Park, it had to be cut off through the insistent voice of a unified faculty unwilling to concede any ground. Acheson decided to develop a bully survey for his math class to learn what the real issues were that needed resolution while teaching a few concepts in range and distribution. "If you make the math relevant by using the concrete example of bullying, you achieve two things at once: (1) They'll get the math, and (2) they'll learn the life lesson that will serve them well long after the math."

What happens in a school culture that is communicated from school leader to faculty and then from the faculty to the students is that the students treat one another as they see the faculty treat one another. Jim Hansen knows (almost) all 1,200 students by name, and everybody knows he's looking out for them. As he walks across campus, he greets every teacher he sees and brings immediately into conversation some issue that is top of mind for that staff member. "It's simple: There's no waffling about what we stand for, and there's nowhere to hide if we don't meet the expectations set for us," Assistant Principal Ken Rocha says, reflecting on Hansen's attention to his community. "We are comfortable in that environment. We experience growth through it, and then provide that same experience for the children."

"Faculty members are genuinely interested in each other as people and as professionals. Our interests not only get taken to the classroom but they get talked about—and the students benefit from that when they see it and learn to become a genuine community of learning," says Lauren Kelly, the other of the two assistant principals and a national examiner for the National Schools of Character program. "The most amazing thing is the sense of family among the faculty," says Kelly. "Any school culture is ultimately formed by that school's strengths. Here it comes from the relationships and community among the faculty."

"As a school, we want successful students who are good. It is the sincere expectation of the faculty that every child will not only achieve as students but be a good person," Kelly concludes. "Here we agree what it means to be a good person in democratic society. If we didn't share that common understanding as a whole faculty, we wouldn't have what you see here."

Again, Jim Hansen remarks with characteristic demure, "What I do best is hire people who fit in this environment."

4

Veritas Preparatory Academy

Phoenix, Arizona

School Information	
2131 East Lincoln Drive Phoenix, AZ 85016 Phone: (602) 263–1128 Fax: (602) 263–7997	Public Charter 322 students Grades 6 through 12 91% white, 5% Hispanic

Cultural Traits Highlighted	Key Practices Featured
• A strong belief that culture determines outcomes	• Great books curriculum • Ongoing seminars for faculty • Shared faculty work space encourages continuous professional development
• A culture committed to student success	• Socratic teaching method encourages rich student–teacher interactions • In-class modeling of ethical behavior
• A culture of people, principles, and purpose	• Faculty recruited from great books colleges • Family handbook details expectations

Ⅰf there is one overarching goal for the leadership team of Great Hearts Academies, a network of six public charter schools that serve the greater Phoenix metropolitan area, it is to utterly transform the American high school and return our educational system to a more rigorous standard of a much earlier time. The founders of Great Hearts are aware that the success of their mission, properly understood, will be measurable only many years from now. That said, they can already say with absolute certainty today that they are making accessible to all a classical education of extraordinarily exacting standards.

More revolutionary still—as these schools openly refer to their mission as *revolutionary*—this focus on the classics is not an escape from modernity but rather a radical commitment to form properly grounded persons who know themselves better and can effectively engage the modern world. It is the moral dimension of this mission, and the school culture required to pull it off, that is perhaps the most revolutionary thing of all.

Early Years

Great Hearts traces its founding to 1996 as a stand-alone charter school called Tempe Preparatory Academy, whose course of instruction was a secularized version of the Catholic curriculum developed by Trinity Schools of South Bend, Indiana.[3] But in many ways, Great Hearts was effectively born in 2003, when Andrew Ellison, founding headmaster of Veritas Preparatory Academy, replicated much of the school culture he had learned as a teacher at Tempe Prep with his school featuring the great books program that is now the core of the Great Hearts model. The following year, Great Hearts Academies was officially formed as Arizona's first nonprofit charter school management organization, and in 2005, Dr. Daniel Scoggin was hired away from the headmastership of Tempe Prep to serve as the CEO of Great Hearts where he is today overseeing the growing network of schools.

It doesn't take long to understand that Great Hearts is serious about its most audacious goal. But what is more disarming, if not equally inspiring, is the simple fact that the transformation of the educational system envisioned by Great Hearts is at root a desire to develop a more just society by getting students to think for themselves.

"There is a deliberate choice in the texts we read that helps form the discussion—without an agenda—that creates greathearted men and women," Scoggin explains. "We want our students to be magnanimous. Here they learn to have a sense of obligation and to see beyond themselves."

Listening to Dan Scoggin and Peter Bezanson, his chief academic officer (himself a graduate of St. John's College, the storied great books school where he goes twice a year to recruit more than ten new teachers annually for their demanding program), you immediately get the sense that there are specific traits that drive Great Hearts' understanding of excellence, traits that are deeply rooted in a cultural sensibility that is slipping away from our everyday experience.

"We deeply value eloquence: a thoughtful use of speech. We are serious about language, about words, and the meaning and ideals of Western culture," Scoggin adds.

Founded as a high school program, Great Hearts is now a system of Grades 6 through 12 schools that promotes in its students a philosophical mind-set that some people would reserve only for the most elite university students—a mindset that lets reason speak for itself.

"If you reason well and argue forcefully, you can discern the truth," Scoggin states plainly. The deep insight here, he argues further, is that freedom and obligation work together in the Western tradition and so his school culture is structured the same way. "We give students the freedom to deeply explore the Western tradition and so discover for themselves their deepest moral obligations."

It may not be immediately apparent to some what is at stake here. Recently, Scoggin (2008) has written,

It is our duty to study the very best expressions of the human condition and our heritage—the achievement of the last three millennia in literature, philosophy, science, math, and the arts. . . . Great Hearts Academies exists for this reason: to support each student's quest to live as a free citizen of the West. . . . The alternative is truly servile. Will we be faced with a generation of young adults who can all read and cipher but who are immediately susceptible to the pounding influence of media, marketing, and propaganda to an extent hitherto unheard of and unimagined? Will we have a generation of young who are technical masters but who cannot refute the most basic of illogical arguments by calling out the suppositions underlying the debate? (p. 22)

A Voice in the Desert

Situated just east of the Phoenix North Mountain Preserve with a school parking lot that abuts the roaring traffic of Arizona Highway 51, Veritas Preparatory Academy occupies a five-day-a-week lease in a sorry church property that is a sad mixture of a low-cost budget and an early 1970s design. "We have no unfair advantage with our facilities," jokes headmaster Andrew Ellison. The strange juxtaposition of the squat church buildings tucked underneath the looming mountain nearby makes a fine comparison, however, to the vitality of the school's students bursting from all sides of a building that makes no effort to contain them. Between classes, neatly uniformed girls actively converse on a balcony overlooking a small desert quadrangle while both boys and girls assemble some impromptu games on a basketball court and an even smaller soccer field adjoining it.

Andrew Ellison still teaches five days a week. On a tiny whiteboard behind his desk in an office that can just barely seat three adults, irregular Latin noun declensions are written out from a ninth-grade tutorial earlier that day. "There is no *choice*—you are going to have a school culture. The question is

Veritas Prep Courtyard in Desert Landscape

do you intentionally create a *good* one? If you do not, by default, your school culture will be heavily influenced by mass media pop culture—these are the waters our students swim in."

With his neatly trimmed reddish beard, tightly drawn suspenders, and exquisite elocution, Ellison seems a throwback to an earlier age. But it doesn't take long for the temptation to peg him as some backward Victorian schoolmaster to wear off. Everybody in this organization somehow seems on fire with their message.

"It would be a *disaster* if we defined ourselves *negatively*," Ellison declares, somehow forcefully biting his words as he comfortably leans back in his desk chair. "Rather, we have to say what we *love*. We love great books, great music, great *discussion*. The great high culture of the West is what we are *for*."

Like Scoggin and Bezanson and the other members of the leadership team back at the corporate office, Ellison artfully lays out his school's mission and vision. He explains how Great Hearts has provided a real, refreshing alternative to the local public school primarily through the quality of its curriculum, the personality of the teachers, and the depth of the relationships the students share with them.

THE GREAT BOOKS CURRICULUM

All students at Veritas, like at all Great Hearts Academies, take no elective subjects. A true classical curriculum, the course of studies at Great Hearts leaves nothing to chance and prescribes exactly what is learned by every student, at every level, in every discipline with one exception: foreign language. All students in Grades 6 through 8 take Latin. A little more than one-third of the student body then continues taking classical language with Latin 3 and 4 in Grades 9 and 10 (Virgil, Horace) and Greek 1 and 2 in Grades 11 and 12 (Homer, Euripides). The other two-thirds of the students (through a four-year immersion approach) take French or Spanish, enabling them in a fluent-speaking environment to read and discuss either Cervantes or Molière by their fourth year.

All students upon graduation will have completed seven years of lab science and seven years of math, including two full years of calculus. All students study the fine arts every year to include music, poetry, studio art, and drama. In the middle school grades, in English, students study literature and composition. In history, they study the American tradition and ancient and medieval history. When the students reach ninth grade, the time spent on English and history is combined into a two-hour Humane Letters seminar every day, five days a week, in which they read and discuss the greatest works of the Western canon. From Lincoln's Second Inaugural, the Constitution of the United States, and selected essays from the Federalist Papers, students learn to analyze for themselves and defend on their own terms the principles of the American founding. By reading through Homer, Virgil, Euripides, Sophocles, and Aristophanes to Dostoevsky, Potok, Cather, Austin, and Crane, they experience for themselves the most beautiful writings of the Western world and learn to discern in conversation what lies hidden in these texts that is as true today as it was when they were first written.

"Everything we teach on its own terms—not in relation to the popular culture. We aim to understand what is happening in the very thing we are studying," Ellison explains. This practical instructional tenet in itself is a powerful witness to the persistent quality and value of what they read at Great Hearts, but it is also an equally important early lesson for the students at Great Hearts in the care, focus, and objectivity that real scholars devote to the subject of their studies. Without compromise, the school culture at Great Hearts is designed to create the environment necessary for its students to experience this level of intellectual seriousness for themselves.

With this, Ellison begins to explain how the curriculum is connected to the personality of the teachers required to facilitate these rich but very demanding classroom conversations.

MASTER TEACHERS

"When students are surrounded by teachers who are highminded and passionate about the true, the good, and the beautiful—the students build habits of longing for fine, lasting, and difficult things." It is with this last and very subtle reference to habits that one notices how very little moralizing goes on at Great Hearts. One is not told to be good, rather one is immersed in an environment in which what it means to be good truly needs to be discerned and then made one's own.

That said, Great Hearts is hardly a free-for-all. Although there may not be a lot of moral or ethical exhortation going on, solid ethical behavior is *constantly* modeled and the school day itself is designed to give students lots of opportunities to practice good habits. As Ellison observes, "A good seminar, for example, is an ethical experience that inculcates good habits of grace in conversation, attentiveness, and intellectual striving."

What appears critical to the success and identity of the school culture at Great Hearts is how through repeated subtle actions students obtain many habits of order and good appearance. Students and teachers alike address one another as Mr. and Ms., which not only creates a professional interaction with a certain air of deference and respect but also it focuses the conversation in the classroom entirely on the ideas at hand—neutralizing the role of personalities in the room—and gives the ideas themselves the room they need to run and infuse the room with new insights.

Humane Letters Seminar Provides the Focal Point for the Discussion of the Great Books

In a ninth-grade Humane Letters seminar, twenty boys and girls are seated around a square table. Facing one another, the students are in the second hour of discussing the National Organization of Women's founding Statement of Purpose from 1966.[4] A question emerges from the teacher regarding the value to society of women being able to raise their children at home versus losing the voice of women in industry. A vigorous, polite, and humorous debate is facilitated by the teacher's prodding. Then one boy presents an argument, citing a discussion from earlier in the year, in which it was maintained that women are more emotional and less rational than men, and so it could be argued that they are better suited by nature to make a more meaningful contribution to society by staying in the home. Citing the document itself, a girl directly across from the boy asks, "Do you not believe that 'it is as essential for every girl to be educated to her full potential of human ability as it is for every boy—with the knowledge that such education is the key to effective participation in today's economy'?" The whole table sits forward, invigorated by the prospect of a good fight. Her interlocutor sits back in his chair "I didn't say you shouldn't be educated—or educated to your full potential—rather, I was suggesting that there won't be much of an economy to participate in, if you aren't back home making babies." The whole class twitters at the sharp retort but immediately realizes that an unacceptable line has been crossed. "Let's not personalize the conversation, Mr. Wilson," the teacher admonishes. "Ms. Rodriguez, continue with this point about education and a person's economic value and be sure to focus it on the question at hand."

Instantly, Ellison's point about the quality of his teachers and the power of the student–teacher relationship comes clearly into view. Their personal dedication to the life of the mind is a daily inspiration to the students, but it has to be in evidence daily for it to be an inspiration. Even more to the point, Ellison's earlier observation about *intellectual striving* is perhaps more true for the teachers than it is for the students if the students are to benefit from how Great Hearts is structured.

"I wouldn't do this in any other environment," Ellison says matter-of-factly. "At Great Hearts I have daily opportunities to be positively shaped and formed myself as we work to shape the culture for our students."

Not surprising, in the same way Great Hearts is structured to inculcate good habits in the students, it is also structured to support the ongoing growth and development of its teachers. Faculty members participate in a mandatory seminar that runs across the school year (three times annually) to discuss a great book and hone their skills for the classroom. Most recently, they read *Persuasion* by Jane Austin and an early essay by Albert Einstein. Again, true to its culture of subtle details of great importance, the faculty members do not have individual classrooms or offices; rather, they share a single faculty office with common desks where they can interact with one another throughout the day, talk instruction, and engage in further inquiry. Ellison notes, "Teachers have to talk to each other constantly if they are to have the real needs of the students in mind and keep their own desire for learning properly stoked."

Personal Relationships

The obvious rigor of the curriculum and the required quality of teaching to pull it off come together to form what may be the very center of Great Hearts' extraordinary school culture: the student–teacher relationship. Dan Scoggin puts it this way, "All teachers need a self-motivating, self-regulating engine, but if you have unhappy teachers, you will have unhappy students." It has been said that great teaching comes from the identity and integrity of teachers, but at Great Hearts the Socratic humility of the teachers who place themselves in the service of the books they read is extraordinarily instructive for the manner in which it brings student and teacher together in a common pursuit of the truth. Scoggin adds, "The Socratic method both allows intelligence to be revered and allows a leveling up of the students to the teacher's level." It is the

Socratic method, in other words, that creates the student-teacher relationship, and it is the power of this relationship that gives the teachers both the moral authority and the confidence to push their students harder in the pursuit of the true, the good, and the beautiful.

The genius in all of this is quite old-fashioned. As the founders of Great Hearts know all too well, this approach is as old as the Western tradition itself. The Greeks understood how a young person develops across his or her education: First learning grammar, then rhetoric, until finally, he or she is ready for philosophy. What Scoggin and others at Great Hearts are quick to point out (in this age of disaffected teenagers to whom the culture at large has successfully sold a message of isolation and alienation) is that the Socratic method is exactly the right method for teaching such young people. "Teenagers because they are so turned in on themselves are naturally inclined to engage the existential search to answer the question who am I?" And it is precisely because teenagers can be dangerously narcissistic that they need both good influences and good reasons not to be focused exclusively on themselves. And here, as Scoggin puts it so elegantly, is Great Hearts' hook: "The best way for students to answer life's deepest questions is to let them answer for themselves in conversation with the great ideas."

Almost without having to say it, it becomes clear how Great Hearts is able to engage personally meaningful ethical conversation without it becoming moralizing. For one, the overall approach emphasizes the Greek tradition, which is both pre-Christian and without religious content, but it is the curriculum as a whole, every day, that gives an external context to any discussion of virtue or vice, so that everyone—student and teacher alike—is free to explore what it means for them.

"If you don't work to intentionally shape your school culture, something is going to fill that vacuum—the shadow culture of what isn't emphasized," Scoggin observes, demonstrating another benefit of Great Hearts' highly prescriptive approach. "We exclude all pop culture without judging it and leave it at the door." Both the neutrality of this posture and the complete lack of equivocation are key to Great Hearts' success on this front. A fifty-page, single-spaced family handbook that is signed by parents and students alike outlines exactly how explicit the school is in its expectations on this and other matters. To encourage genuine reflection on the great high culture of the West, all distractions have to be eliminated. And as Scoggin points out, "What most defines a free human being is what they think and how they treat others—not what they wear."

However timeless this truth may be, it is nonetheless a radical concept today and one that takes a great deal of coordinated and focused activity to assert. Unlike the great balance of public schools in America, Great Hearts purposely works to make sure their students do not, as Peter Bezanson ominously puts it, "Get trapped on an island of modern self-creation." Rather, they require their faculty to be authentic models of human striving for their students to emulate. The simple truth they stand behind is that students who are openly engaged in profound discussion will find the truth without it being forced on them—more important, they'll make it their own because they will have found it for themselves.

Veritas Students Practicing Their Choral Arts

In the basement of the church building that houses Veritas Prep, Laura Inman, who has a doctorate from Arizona State University in choral conducting and is herself a six-year veteran of the Phoenix Chorale—recently nominated for three Grammys in multiple categories[5]—is asked by the headmaster if her students might be willing to sing. Without any preparation the tenth graders stand up, tuck in their uniforms, clear their throats, and wait for Dr. Inman's signal. From memory, they proceed to sing, rather beautifully, a sixteenth-century Italian madrigal by Orlando di Lasso, the great Franco-Flemish composer of the late Renaissance. One can only imagine the impact such singing must have when it is performed for their parents who get an immediate and visceral experience not only of the beautiful but also of their child's excellent education and individual personal formation.

The Western tradition is key to Great Hearts' identity and excellence. Does it have to be the Western tradition? "No," Scoggin replies, "but students need to understand their own tradition first if they are to learn how to adequately engage another. But I could easily see Great Hearts Chinese Academy, Beijing."

5

Hinsdale Central High School

Hinsdale, Illinois

School Information	
55th and Grant Streets Hinsdale, IL 60521 Phone: (630) 570–8000	Public 2,624 students Grades 9 through 12 81% white, 12% Asian, 4% Hispanic, 3% black

Cultural Traits Highlighted	Key Practices Featured
• A nurturing but demanding culture	• Proudly competitive environment • Environment respectful of differences • Trusting relationships
• A culture committed to student success	• Peer leaders assigned to all freshmen • Ambassadors acclimate transfer students • Break Down the Walls
• A culture of people, principles, and purpose	• Student-led cultural change • Faculty teams support cultural change

To say that Hinsdale Central High School is a sports giant is a gross understatement. For generations this sports behemoth known as "The Home of the Red Devils" has dominated its opponents in local, state, and national competition while fielding more than thirty separate athletic teams. If high school sports at their best are intended to act on teenagers like a purifying fire—the way gold is tried in a furnace—then Hinsdale Central is itself the inferno.

On any given Friday, the entire school is ablaze. Every man, woman, and child—nearly 2,700 students and more than 200 faculty members committed to their care—are dressed almost entirely in red. Red and white banners dating back to 1909 hang from every square foot of the gymnasium proclaiming countless state and national titles as if to say to the opposing squad, *abandon hope all ye who enter here.* Framed team photographs, laid one against the next, line both sides of every corridor in the school. The sports photos in the hallways only stop for the floor-to-ceiling glass-covered trophy cases—dozens of them—that run throughout the entire building. "It's more our spirit than the sports that makes us so special," says Andrea Robinson, a senior on track-and-field and gymnastics teams

Home of the Red Devils Featuring State Titles Dating Back to 1909

and the varsity spirit club. "We fill up stadiums on both sides. There are fans everywhere here for every sport and club."

Down the hallway, you can hear the roar of the field house: maximum occupancy—1,702. No one else is allowed in today. The din of the fans is deafening. Like the banners in the gym, the walls of the field house are painted with massive murals listing year after year the West Suburban Conference Titles and state top finishes that Hinsdale has won in almost every sport imaginable. You can see for yourself that the girls' varsity tennis team has won the Illinois state championships twenty-seven times *since 1973*. What you might not know is this year, one team player, Courtney Dolehide, opted out of the high school tennis season to play in the United States Open instead.

TEAM SPIRIT

In the midst of this unrelenting competition and communal pursuit of excellence, what is most remarkable about Hinsdale is the joy and cheerfulness that so characterizes the student body. In so many local public high schools, but especially in well-heeled communities where competition of this kind is celebrated, competition can become cruel, and among the young, it can be brutal.[6] Make no mistake, the marquee athletes, the cheerleaders, and the girls on the dance squad all walk like giants at Central, but you notice immediately when you meet them in person that their mission is not to dwarf the others, but to lift everyone up.

"We're known for how we treat our freshman," says Adrienne Walker, a senior who is in more clubs than most students have subjects in their course load. "We want them to join our clubs, and we work especially hard to recruit them." This is not so much talk from a good kid but a fact that has been institutionalized in the culture of the school. At the recommendation of the students, the freshman start the first day of school by themselves so they can get the lay of the land before its gets overwhelmed by others more familiar with the landscape. Peer leaders are assigned to every new freshman student, and

Hinsdale Cheerleaders Fire Up the Red Devil Crowd

ambassadors are assigned to new transfer students to help them get acclimated. The student body as a whole is committed to no student ever sitting alone at lunch. On the first day of school, the entire student council arrives before the freshmen and "claps them into class" with a standing ovation that runs throughout the school corridors. "The transition from eighth grade to ninth is the hardest for everyone," says Peter Garcia, a varsity football player and member of several student organizations. "Here, we've just figured out how to make it easier."

It was not always this way at Hinsdale. In February 1982, two students committed suicide in a single week. Years later, in 1998, another student took his life. The accepted truth at the school today is that the culture was so cruel that this latter child was literally bullied into killing himself.

This was during the post-Columbine era when schools all across the country were first reflecting on the many causes of student alienation that is increasingly in evidence among so many young people.

Pam Bylsma arrived at Hinsdale during the 1999–2000 school year from Plainfield High where she was Dean of

Students. Under her leadership, an exploratory committee pursued a yearlong study with the goal to "improve school culture in an atmosphere of growth and change." By 2001, the entire school community embraced a comprehensive long-term initiative to "reculture our school."

Team Turnaround

In addressing this challenge, Pam Bylsma speaks of two schools: "The school the adults see and the school the students live in." Although many school leaders acknowledge there can be a big difference between what is explicitly taught in school and what students implicitly learn throughout the school day, Bylsma's accomplishment runs deeper for her insistence that the solution to Hinsdale's very real cultural problems had to come from the students themselves. "We wanted to change the very culture they were operating in by responding to the root causes of their concern." The key to getting this done was twofold: (1) activating students to discuss what matters to them and (2) providing authentic leadership opportunities for them to resolve their concerns. According to this approach, only the students can surface the real issues as they experience them. As a consequence, the solutions they come up with are often rather surprising in form—but even more surprising in their effectiveness.

One of the most popular and most respected organizations on campus today is a student-led, student-founded club to prevent bullying called Break Down the Walls. "In middle school, the popular kids are the bullies," says Mark Malkoski, a junior. "Because they don't yet know who they are—their insecurity lashes out," he observes almost clinically and yet somehow with the warmth and innocence of a child. "When they get noticed for it, they only do it more." To break the vicious cycle of children 'growing up' at each other's expense, the members of Break Down the Walls develop a skit each year that helps define and illustrate what bullying is in explicit terms that the students will not only find relevant but life-changing. The most harmful bullying

Breaking Down the Walls Dramatizes Mean Girls Ganging Up on a Peer During Lunch

many students observe is a lot more verbal or even psychological than usually conceived—attacking children where they can be hurt the most, which is often where they have the greatest need to grow. Bullying left unchecked not only deforms the bully, but it can also leave a lot of stunted growth behind. Because of this, the faculty admits that the skits can be edgy if not downright raw, but members of the club say they have to use language or images that would never be condoned in class if they are to make their point. "It's necessary to show it like it is—while making it entertaining—because these topics are hard to look at," says Emma Carroll, an active member of Break Down the Walls and several other clubs in addition to her leadership positions on the water polo and gymnastics teams.

Over the years, this student organization that is designed to break down the walls that artificially alienate students from one another has not only become a cultural hallmark of the school but also of the larger community.[7] Private and religious schools from five different communities feed into Hinsdale Central including fourteen public middle schools. Break Down the Walls now travels throughout the region and state spreading its message while the middle schools they visit have formed similar groups now performing skits of their own at elementary schools in the area. If it was bullying and social intimidation that brought Central to its darkest hour, the intentional effort to prevent bullying is now helping to heal the whole community from within.

By many reports, whether from alumni or parents of past students, Hinsdale Central was not a pleasant place to come of age in the 1980s or 1990s. "In the 1980s, this was a mean school and not a nice place to be," admits George Miller, who has been teaching at Hinsdale Central for thirty-three years. "You did not feel welcome in the building, but especially if you weren't from the right country club."

Mary Buddig is the current PTO president, an alumna of the school, and a parent with two children at Hinsdale and three others who have recently graduated. "When I came here you didn't tell your friends what you were trying out for because you didn't want to get knocked out—competition was everything." She continues, "Now it's just different—it's about mutual respect and giving it your personal best." Mary Kiser agrees. "It was not a kind environment," she states plainly. "Students joined clubs for their college resumes. Now, they really give of themselves and are encouraged to give more out of a culture of respect."

LEADING CHANGE

How Hinsdale achieved such widespread cultural change is very instructive. "If you want something sustainable, it requires a grassroots effort that is maintained through regular reflection," says Stephanie Palmer who has been an assistant principal alongside Pam Bylsma for the last three years. "Pam is low-key, and she knows it is not about her—she just wants the results," Stephanie observes. "But you need a Pam," adds Pam Kalafut, the student activities director and a key member of the leadership team that made these changes possible. "Pam has the time, the energy, the passion, and the universal view needed to bring all the departments together."

Three faculty teams were formed to lead the programmatic changes needed to embed a new culture across student life, the curriculum, and the school's broader connection with the surrounding community.[8] As Pam Bylsma says, "Once you allow individuals to discover their potential to positively shape the culture, they will never again want to go back to being a passive member of the school community." But Bylsma also had the support of the school's principal, James Ferguson, who she says took five critical actions to get their work off the ground so her teams could help reculture the school:

1. He set aside time for meetings on every professional development day and made it sacred so no other initiative or department could touch it.

2. He told the department chairs to support the initiative and assign a teacher to each collaborative team.

3. He required a work goal every year related to the initiative for all certified staff.

4. He did not let a lack of outside funding kill the initiative, but found a way to fund it.

5. He invited every community organization he could to informational meetings and explained that the school

needed to partner with them to be successful. The more good news that became public, the more enthused the community became.

Besides distributing ownership of the school culture across a larger number of people, Hinsdale shows that school culture ultimately has to be more process driven if you want it to be sustainable and lasting. At Hinsdale Central, the key process appears to be

listen to the students ➜ help them take action ➜ reflect on the results ➜ listen to the students again and get more feedback.

"What is very different about Central," says Lisa Bucciarelli, the team leader in charge of student life, "is the degree to which we actively seek out the students' voices." She continues, saying, "Once you see the data and the results, it's inspirational and you get passionate about it." The virtuous cycle that is created once the faculty members listen to the students and build genuine relationships founded on meeting their individual needs is unmistakable. "Students get engaged once they see for themselves that you are serious about them," says Bill Walsh, a dean of the school and the team leader responsible for integrating the school's cultural changes across the curriculum. "The more students are involved, the more pride they develop in their school." That said, there is no way to overstate exactly how involved these students are in the life of their school.

The mantra at Hinsdale is quite simple: If there isn't a club for what you're interested in—then start one. Again, no one goes it alone at Central, we're all in this together.

At last count, the school's official "Clubs at A Glance" flyer listed contact information and meeting locations for eighty-four separate student-led clubs. As Emma Carroll says, "There are so many clubs and leadership opportunities that everyone has a chance to *really* help in a *real* way." When you hear that in addition to the demanding academic schedule

and a full-time commitment to sports, most students participate in as many as five clubs each, you want to ask—where
does all this energy come from? "It comes from loving where
you are," Adrienne Walker answers without hesitation. "You
are so *refreshed* by the other people around you, you simply
apply yourself more." Or as Tomi Adeyemi says, "What
makes this school so great is that we each have the opportunity to truly be ourselves."

In a room full of students representing the broadest array
of school sports and activities, the conversation as a whole is
characterized by a level of maturity and self-assurance that
would be completely disarming if the scene itself weren't so
genuine. All of the students, taken both individually and as a
group, are so comfortable speaking openly, you actually experience in the moment the forward momentum and creative
force of honest conversation.

I think to ask, what can other schools learn from Hinsdale?
"The student body often gets a lot of credit for what goes on
here, but the easiest place to start is with the teachers," Tomi
declares with a depth of insight well beyond her years. "You
can't immediately change the surrounding community. And
students unaided won't set goals for themselves on their own.
But if an adult cares for you and believes in you—you learn
you can do anything."

"Goals matter," says Teddy Vernon, a senior and the
copresident of the citizen club. "When you see students from
other schools, the ones who are lost haven't decided where
they're going. Here, we pride ourselves on our school and our
education, and that's a huge advantage, but no matter where
you are, if you set goals for yourself, you can accomplish anything." Just listening to them, you begin to hear a pattern.

While goals certainly matter, especially in driving high performance, Hinsdale's experience demonstrates with absolute certainty that trusting relationships must come first. "People go into
education out of a love for children; when they forget that and
focus on content instead—they lose the connection required to
teach that content," Pam Bylsma declares. In great school cultures,

relationships really matter—and when the task at hand is the turnaround of a school culture that has poisoned itself, relationships matter much more than both content area expertise or outstanding teaching technique.

Bylsma uses the data from the many surveys she performs to demonstrate this to her teachers. Kristi Frost, a veteran chemistry teacher, is but one example. "My focus over the last ten years has gone from the curriculum to the students themselves," she says. The impact of Frost's approach—whether in the classroom or outside it—is nicely illustrated in a recent project called "Red Goes Green," through which the Red Devil community was able to reduce the institution's total postconsumer waste by one-third in a single year. "When you focus on the student, the level of engagement soars," she says. "Or looked at another way, once a community trusts itself enough to openly confront its deepest individual needs, improving trash collection becomes a breeze."[9]

RELATIONSHIPS THAT INSPIRE

In a group discussion with several members of the faculty, the challenge to understand what Hinsdale has accomplished and what it can teach other schools is taken to a whole new level. "The relationships the staff members have with the students is the number one strength of this school—in the clubs and in the classroom," says Jim Kupres, social worker and boys track coach. But given Hinsdale's focus on human relationships to inspire excellence in others—even if that relationship is given great priority—it is what is *modeled* that drives achievement, and so what is modeled must also be excellent. What exactly does that require of the faculty?

"This is a very competitive school, so integrity has always been a concern of the faculty," says Bill Walsh. "Win at all costs versus win with integrity is the challenge at hand. We have parents who make excuses for their students—who will even lie for their kids—overcoming that can only come from a culture that can give them more."

Deep within these words is a truth that students at Hinsdale seem to experience now on a massive scale. When it is everyman for himself, only one man wins. And yet when it is all for one and one for all, everyone can win. Actually *everyone*. Again, this now appears to be a lesson that the students, guided by the faculty, are teaching the broader community—including, at times, some of their parents.

"How you express yourself defines who you are," Walsh notes. "The students here want to be good, and they want to do well. The playing field isn't the only thing, it's the *community* they are a part of that they want, and they *realize* they can't have that on their own." It is the depth of this realization and how it is internalized by the students at Hinsdale that is so edifying, but perhaps most especially for the adults in the community.

Both faculty and alumni tell stories of an earlier time not so long ago when Hinsdale fans used to dress in white trash bags when hosting football teams from across the tracks. In force, as a community, they were comfortable calling their opponents "white trash." More recently, during this past football season, the rival fans of the opposing team apparently were relentless in their jeering and name-calling throughout the length of the game. Hinsdale Central students meanwhile cheered their team on refusing to take the bait. At one point, two loud Hinsdale fans tried to get their crowd to return the favor by bringing out some name-calling of their own, but when they weren't immediately joined by their fellow students, their thankless voices simply faded away.

For some, the story of Hinsdale Central High School will have little to say to them because so many of the students and their families come from so much. To think this, however, in an age of flagrant corruption demonstrated in gross variety by countless social elites is to miss entirely the sweeping implications of Hinsdale's basic commitment to the good. As Pam Bylsma remarks, "Affluent children often have far more complex social difficulties and greater challenges with ethical issues than children from homes with fewer resources." Or as John Naisbitt, social studies teacher and boys' varsity tennis coach, counters with some defiance, "I refuse to be dismissed because we are from an affluent community. It is the caring, the commitment, and the energy of this school that makes us different."

What is so remarkable about the character of the community that Hinsdale Central has become is the manner in which their striving for excellence reveals how genuine human goodness can overcome what is often experienced in highly competitive environments as the "achievement dilemma."

In high-performing organizations, among individuals performing the same function, any one individual can be ranked dead last—relative to her peers—no matter how high achieving that individual may be. It is through this mechanism that many great organizations foster competition and accelerate achievement, but it is also through this mechanism that many people—even natural competitors—become demoralized, experience humiliation, or, collapsing under the pressure of that same competition, make bad ethical choices and begin to cheat in the effort to win at all costs.

At Hinsdale this natural, brutal aspect of competition has been engaged openly to create a community so concerned with the success of everyone—but so committed to genuine achievement—that it has *broadened* the reach of Red Devil excellence into every imaginable corner of activity. As Bill Walsh again explains, "Not everyone can be number one when so many are so great, but here that opens up tons of opportunity for students to make connections or to achieve in another way that they haven't thought of before." Several highly competitive boys openly admit how true this was for them. When John Whitelaw, with his 5.0 GPA, started as the varsity quarterback his sophomore year, a number of boys went looking elsewhere for teams to lead. One boy jokes, "Our drama, our wrestling, maybe even our math team are better off this year because we knew Whitelaw couldn't be beat."

It would be easy to miss a lot of these subtleties at first glance. Walking down the hallway during the transition period between classes at Hinsdale can be an intimidating event for even the most experienced school watcher. Hundreds upon hundreds of students pour from every door into four square hallways that make no effort to channel the carefree enthusiasm or raucous conversation of a sea of teenagers dressed in every casual fashion under the sun. Hats of every kind are worn forward and backward, shorts of every length—even pajamas—are in evidence, while, most incredibly, dozens and dozens of the salmon swimming upstream listen to iPods during the course of the conversations they carry out. In minutes, however, the hallways empty, silence returns, and these same students can be seen through the windows of their classroom doorways leaning forward, engaged now in the lesson at hand.

"The school's reputation from the outside is that the inmates are running the asylum—the hats, the shorts, the iPods," says Tom Paulsen, one of two interim principals who came out of retirement to work at Central during the search for a new head of school. "But the truth is the kids are so responsive because they are so respected by the adults in this building."

"There is not a culture here that the administration has to put rules in place to stem bad behavior," Stephanie Palmer, the assistant principal for instruction, explains. "Rather, we treat every issue on an individual student basis." The immensity of what this really means as an operational challenge for the administration cannot be overstated. Nor can you overstate Hinsdale's success in achieving its own brand of order.

On any given day, for example, across the master schedule, it is possible for the student body to accumulate 9,000 tardies. Early in the school year, the administration recorded forty-eight tardies one day and worked immediately to reduce that number. "As administrators we change the focus of what the students are doing and why they're doing it away from themselves and on to others or to larger goals that we all share," Stephanie explains. "Meanwhile, the faculty focuses on the individual student, so the individual issue is addressed individually." By tying their schoolwide effort to eliminate tardies to the academic success of each and every individual student in the building, the total daily number of tardies went from forty-eight to thirteen to three over the course of that same week.

Again, at Hinsdale Central, we're all in this together.

And we like to win—together.

6

Osmond A. Church School

P.S./M.S. 124
South Ozone Park, New York

School Information	
129–15 150th Avenue South Ozone Park, NY 11420 Phone: (718) 529–2580	Public 1,143 students Kindergarten through Grade 8 40% Asian, 36% black, 21% Hispanic, 3% white
Cultural Traits Highlighted	**Key Practices Featured**
• A strong belief that culture determines outcomes • A nurturing but demanding culture • A culture committed to student success	• Core Knowledge curriculum • Core Virtues curriculum • Focus on human outcomes • Promote intelligent risk taking • Strong sense of family between and among students and faculty

The enormous transatlantic jets that land on runway twelve into Kennedy International Airport fill the entire window of Valarie Lewis's office just before they touch down some 300 feet ahead—as if the school itself were parked on the airfield. On a sunny day, with the windows open, the noise can be deafening. The aircrafts approach approximately every two minutes.

The whole scene is a study in contrasts. While the world's eighteenth busiest airport roars outside, the inside of Valarie's office could double as a Victorian curiosity shop: warm, cozy, and inviting. Colorful oddities and other conversation pieces hang from dozens of makeshift shelves—the entire affair dominated by the largest and most eccentric teapot collection you have ever seen. You get the immediate impression that you could learn quite a lot in so comfortable and intriguing a room. You literally have no idea that you are in the principal's office of a New York City public school.

Just outside the office, a small army of administrative support staff work the phones, attend to parents, and amid a wall-to-wall installation of military-issue filing cabinets manage mountains of bureaucratic documents they have to comply with daily. In the midst of this scene, one middle school girl is being gently corrected for wearing tight-fitting jeans that are torn in patches. With a hand placed on each of the girl's shoulders and a compassionate look of deep concern in her eyes, one staff member says, "This may be the fashion on the street, but this is not for you. Bring only the best kind of attention to yourself." The girl smiles warmly, returning the deep gaze with what appears to be a grateful look on her face, as if somehow the entire exchange had actually occurred in private.

EDUCATIONAL OASIS

Like all New York City public schools, the Osmond A. Church School has the forbidding badged officers at the entranceway, the caged metal staircases, and those absurdly loud bells more fitting in a penal institution, but once you see the colors (Lord

Almighty, the bright colors in the hallways!), the quality of student work on the walls, and the raw instructional horsepower in evidence in every classroom, you know immediately that you have arrived someplace very special.

Hallway Features Fourth-Grade Core Knowledge Unit on China

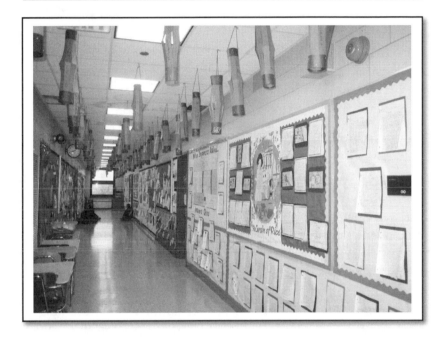

Ninety-four percent of the students at P.S. 124 come from low-income families, but more than eight percent of these are housed in homeless shelters, and even more come from foster homes. For many of these children, school is the only safe place they have. When you speak with them individually, what they most value about their school is how safe and secure they feel here. In their minds, having the armed security guards on campus is a net positive. But the deeper sense of security they experience comes from the greater opportunity that is being afforded to them, which they know is not available to many students in the neighboring schools.[10]

"When kids run around in school, it isn't fun, it's scary," one boy says rather neutrally, making his observation all the more precocious. "Our teachers work us hard here, but they never give up on us. More than anything else, it's the teachers that make this school special," says a girl next to him.

In this teacher-driven environment, students at P.S. 124 outperform their peers citywide in both math and English language arts at all grade levels—ninety-nine percent are proficient or advanced in seventh-grade math compared to eighty-one percent passing citywide. Ninety-six percent are proficient or advanced in sixth-grade language arts compared to seventy-three percent across the city (New York State Education Department, 2009). Only in 2005 did P.S. 124 even add these middle school grades. Now, most of the students participate in the Advance Regents Program and prepare for admission to "the exam schools" and the other high-end high school options across the city.

South Ozone Park, where the school is located, is a neighborhood in the southwestern section of the New York City borough of Queens. It was originally developed in the early 1900s as low-cost housing that was added to the more upscale—and at the time rural—community of Ozone Park. Today it is bound by the Aqueduct Racetrack on the west and the Van Wyck Expressway to the east. After other first-generation immigrants like Germans, Irish, and Italians made the neighborhood their own and then left, recent population shifts have made it one of the fastest-growing and most ethnically diverse communities in all of New York City. The students in the school come from Latin America, South America, the West Indies, and Northern Africa. Most recently, a surge of students has come from the south Asian countries of Bangladesh, India, and Pakistan as can be seen from the large number of boys wearing the Sikh turban or *patka* that keeps their ritually uncut hair knotted on the top of their heads.

Valarie Lewis first came to P.S. 124 twenty years ago serving variously as a teacher and grant writer. In 2000, she was elevated to assistant principal under Elaine Thompson and, for the last four years, has herself been the school's principal, glad to have Thompson come back from time to time to see how the school is improving under her successor's tenure.

HUMAN OUTCOMES

Like the decorations in her office and the brightly painted school she runs, Lewis is herself a colorful personality. Practical, well-spoken, and commanding in speech, it is no surprise to learn that she returned to education after successfully owning and operating a business of some scale in the children's clothing industry. A great deal of personal experience seems to inform her vision of the school's ultimate mission.

"The human outcome we're looking for far exceeds the academic outcome," Lewis declares. "Academics will only take them so far."

The irony in this is that P.S. 124 has become a very academic place. When Lewis first arrived she went into 29 classes a week to see and experience for herself the fragmentation across the curriculum that invariably led to poor results. The students were scoring in the thirtieth and fortieth percentile in English language arts. It was at that time that the school made the commitment to the Core Knowledge curriculum and today is recognized as one of the finest implementations of that program in the nation [11] As for the immigrant populations, what better way to be enculturated into American society than to be exposed to the great ideas of the Western world?

"Content is critical. People can learn to think critically only if they have knowledge of real content first," Lewis says in support of the Core Knowledge approach. "But the challenge for us is way past content knowledge. We need to shape students *as people* who can *do* something with it."

The force of this observation has to do with the extraordinary teacher–student relationship Lewis expects to see in every student–teacher interaction. Even given the school's tremendous focus on quality instruction, a greater priority at P.S. 124 appears to be placed on the human connection required to make learning desirable before it can be made meaningful. The reality at P.S. 124 is that the outside culture is so at odds with what the children are taught at school that the school culture itself must overcome the general tenor of society.

"We are a *Core Virtues* school.[12] We do all the standard things like 'virtue of the month,' but that is just icing if you don't *live* it," Lewis says emphatically. "The culture of the building needs to offer a stability that the students don't have on their own."

The lesson here is that children need to believe in their personal value and need to experience what they are worth in the classroom. "We get them to reflect on the choices they make and the people they want to become," Lewis explains. "If they are trained to be freethinkers, they'll come to understand the power of their choices and they'll learn to make better ones for themselves. But to do this, they need to know that we believe in them first. If we develop children to be thinkers and to take chances, we'll have a future. If not, we won't."

There is another irony here in that P.S. 124 is widely admired and often emulated for its "character program." And yet Lewis is quick to dissociate herself from that as well. "It isn't character; it is *understanding* that you're looking for. The real question is how can education help overcome simple prejudice. The communities these children live in can be fiercely segregated. It all comes down to people being able to communicate and understand across differences."

To fulfill its most basic mission as a place of learning, P.S. 124 has learned that it must engage a deeper problem. What is on offer has little to do with values education or the tools of conflict resolution; rather, the school provides a real education in the facts of the human condition. It is *real* in two ways: (1) because it is anchored in rich subject area content and (2) because this rich content is taught in a way that deeply and positively forms the human person.

Knowing is not the same thing as doing. It was Aristotle who first famously taught that "we are what we do repeatedly and so excellence must be a habit." For us to know what to do—and to do what we know is right—we need to practice both. At P.S. 124, the habits of the mind are so regularly matched with habits of the heart that the children have a genuine opportunity both to learn what is good and how to do the right thing. A few examples might help illustrate this point.

On one day in September, when the school as a whole is concentrating on the virtues of respect and responsibility, seventeen kindergartners discuss what it means to be selfish as they read aloud Marcus Pfister's *Rainbow Fish*—that's a whole lot more than simply learning to share as in most kindergartens. Meanwhile next door, a large class of more than 30 first graders tries to distinguish acts of kindness from other signs of respect. "Is it always kind to be respectful?" one girl asks. Suddenly, a very practical conversation breaks out, and the children begin to list the things they can do to show kindness or respect to others and then contrast the two lists. Although shades of gray emerge in the conversation, knowing what it means to be respectful and doing what it takes to show respect begin to come together in a concrete and meaningful way.

Farther down the hall, students in the second grade work independently in five separate groups preparing team projects on the geography of various world deserts. Students record in their notebooks the specific learning objectives they aim to accomplish through each of their assignments. What's the point of students writing out learning objectives? I ask them. Isn't that for the teachers to keep track of? "We need to know what we are doing in order to do it well," one girl explains smiling. The brightly colored classrooms are jammed packed with the artifacts of projects recently completed. The well-spoken students will eagerly chat with you about any of it.

The level of student discipline throughout the school is observably very high. Far from taxing student morale, it appears to drive it. In another second-grade classroom, Mrs. Seith makes a single command and all of her students are sitting on the floor in a matter of moments ready to take up a discussion of art. "The classroom routines have been in place since kindergarten," she notes of the effortless transition, "but the order in the classroom really comes from the culture of the building."

Later that day, in a discussion with other faculty members, I ask her to elaborate on what she meant by "the culture of the building." "The administration sets the tone for the teachers, and the teachers set the tone for the students," Seith remarks. "The children know what is expected of them throughout the building, and they know they are expected to achieve it. That is our culture." She then continues with a key observation reiterated by any number of her colleagues: "Whenever it doesn't happen, whenever a basic expectation is not met, we focus on the individual child, not on the expectation. We talk to the *child* to learn what's missing."

Linda Malloy, the assistant principal, takes this observation a bit further. "Our staff is special: The children do what is expected because they know they are cared for—and they take that home with them." This last comment echoes something Valarie Lewis said earlier that gets to the heart of what P.S. 124 has set out to accomplish. "In dealing with the whole child—you're dealing with the whole family," Lewis concludes. "It is the fragmentation of the family and the dysfunction in society that requires us to stabilize that for them."

Strikingly, many parents at P.S. 124 agree that a good deal of the order in their home comes from what their children learn at the school, and they do not see that as overreaching

P.S. 124 Faculty Members in Core Knowledge Resource Room

on the school's part. One father in particular strongly argues that it is precisely the role of the school to have an identity to which its constituents are expected to conform. "You need to shape the home and shape the families if you want your school to be of a certain shape," Fizul Khan says. The challenge in this last statement is that most educators know this is true, and yet they are either unable to act on it or unwilling to accept the massive responsibility implied. What P.S. 124 and many other schools like it teach us is that teachers themselves cannot be blamed for this circumstance, but it does require them to work together to overwhelm the problem at hand. Teachers know the profound impact that schooling can have on an individual. Most educators, in fact, enter into teaching precisely because they desire meaningful work that can affect children positively. The reality, however, is that when the demand for this level of influence is scaled beyond a few children or beyond a classroom to embrace the whole of a school, the courage to assume this responsibility wanes or the teamwork required to bring it into being collapses under the weight of other priorities not focused so directly on the needs of children. This is not to place blame on any teachers, but rather to point out that the answer lies at the *school* level.

If schools today are seriously challenged to address the dysfunctions in society, it just may be dysfunctions in the school system that make these challenges all the more difficult to address at the local school level. P.S. 124 demonstrates that for a school to serve children well, it matters who teaches, what they teach, and what environment they teach in. The policy implications of this last observation are tremendous as very few school leaders have total control over these three dimensions of their work.

However harsh this may sound—as far as Valarie Lewis is concerned—very few of the New York City Department of Education mandates have *anything* to do with positive human outcomes. Again, a few examples might help illustrate this point: Compliance demands are not aligned to the school design and so do not drive quality; instructional mandates dictated by the city are at odds with others demanded by the state, and together neither elevates whole areas of programmatic weakness; required assessments are not an accurate measure of student progress and hardly a measure at all of student content knowledge; the manner in which progress is reported varies so often as to lose all utility; zoning requirements do not invite feeder schools to be instructional partners with their receiving schools; hiring practices, pay scales, and tenure do not reward, encourage, or inspire teachers to constantly improve.

What advice does Lewis have for so many instructional leaders who find themselves in the same spot? "We need freedom from the mandates. I run this school like a charter school. I don't agonize over the reports. Your time is better spent agonizing over the staff," she replies. This is not so much bravado from an accomplished principal. This is an accomplished principal who is concerned that the system has lost its way. [13]

"People know what they should do for children, but they are directed differently. They do their jobs as they have been told," Lewis notes as a matter of fact. But in her mind, the consequences of this behavior are far more sweeping than most people admit, "Everyone suffers because *they lose who they are in the process.*"

Lewis means this last comment as an existential fact. Schools are meant to be places where children thrive. When anything else becomes the focus of a school, the whole enterprise is put at risk. "Even if it is not within you, you have to reach out to every child every day," Lisa Seith remarks. "Children reflect the environment their teachers create. Above all else, they need to know—every day—that we see something good in them."

The staff members speak of Lewis as a very compassionate leader who treats them with empathy and understanding that allows them to do the same with their children.

"I'm not the leader they follow—rather we're in it together. It is more like a *family,*" Lewis concludes. "We care for each other. We have a shared responsibility for each other and to keep these children secure. As a model, it is more like a family than anything else."

While performing the research for this book—across hundreds of interviews—parents, students, teachers, and administrators alike described their school as most like a *family.* More than any other single word, great schools with rich school cultures that aim to form people deeply were described as families. Whenever I pushed back, they would always push back harder, but perhaps nowhere more than at P.S. 124.

"Calling our school a family might be a truism," Ms. Dailey reflects. "But maybe the world needs to come around to the realization that we all have to look after our brothers." A young sixth grader put it even more simply: "It makes sense to me to call this school a family because this is where I feel at home."

7

Providence
St. Mel

Chicago, Illinois

School Information	
119 S. Central Park Boulevard Chicago, IL 60624 Phone: (773) 722–4600 Fax: (773) 722–9004	Private 650 students Kindergarten through Grade 12 99% black, 1% Hispanic or white
Cultural Traits Highlighted	**Key Practices Featured**
• A strong belief that culture determines outcomes	• Mission statement
• A nurturing but demanding culture	• Tough love approach founded on respect for the dignity of all persons
• A culture committed to student success	• Highly disciplined schoolwide routines

At Providence St. Mel, we believe.

We believe in the creation of inspired lives produced by the miracle of hard work.

We are not frightened by the challenges of reality, but believe that we can change our conception of this world and our place within it.

So we work, plan, build, and dream—in that order.

We believe that one must earn the right to dream.

Our talent, discipline, and integrity will be our contribution to a new world, because we believe that we can take this place, this time, and this people, and make a better place, a better time, and a better people.

With God's help, we will either find a way or make one.

—*Providence St. Mel*
Mission Statement

When Barack Obama was sworn in as the forty-fourth President of the United States of America, the Officer-in-Charge of the presidential platform at the U.S. Capitol was Major Gregory L. Canty, a United States Army Officer and an alumnus of Providence St. Mel.

Major Canty was hand selected by the Presidential White House Military Office to serve in this capacity during the inauguration to ensure that the peaceful transfer of power so supremely celebrated between U.S. presidents was executed with the precision, grace, and dignity that the solemn occasion demands. Canty did not disappoint.

A former senior Army White House Social Aide to President George W. Bush, Canty performed his function flawlessly. On that momentous day that many people saw as a fulfillment of a promise first conceived during the civil rights movement of the 1960s, Major Canty was the dignified young black man who orchestrated the proceedings as another young black man was sworn in as the leader of the free world.

Major Gregory L. Canty Saluting President Barack Obama on Inaugural Platform

Alumni like Major Canty are very important to Providence St. Mel. Every year a number of them return to the school for career day, when they share their personal success stories with the whole student body. "This way, the students can see for themselves what great good has come of other people who sat in their very same seats," says Kevin McGrath, a member of the middle school and the high school science department. And the alumni are an impressive bunch—Major Canty is not alone. Without exception, they are poised, disciplined, and very wellspoken. Those who return for career day usually have one or more graduate degrees under their belts and a series of professional accomplishments ready to share with the students. They are proud of their connection to Providence St. Mel and speak very fondly of their experiences there. But deep within all of them, there is something more: a passion for what they have done matched to a sober awareness of what they had to overcome.

As they proclaim in the school's mission statement, theirs are inspired lives produced by the miracle of hard work.

Providence St. Mel is a nondenominational private Christian school located in the east Garfield Park area of

Chicago. It serves 650 students in Grades preK through 12. Seventy percent of the students come from within a three-mile radius of the school, the infamous West Side of Chicago, where in District 11 alone it is not uncommon for the neighborhood to witness a murder a day. Nearly 100% of the student body is black, and almost eight out of ten are raised in single-parent families. Seventy percent qualify for the federal free lunch program and cannot afford the modest tuition that the school charges. These difficult circumstances notwithstanding, for the past thirty years, *100%* of the graduating class has been accepted to four-year colleges. In the last seven years, more than half of these graduates have matriculated to top-tier universities and other institutions of higher learning. Last year's graduating class alone received more than $4.5 million in scholarships to attend the colleges of their choice.

"Every day we tell them, 'We're going to break the cycle of poverty with *you*,'" says Adrienne Turner, longtime math teacher and head of the math department. "When it happens, when they come back on career day to show what's happened to them, they credit the mission statement as showing them the way."

Julie Jovan, the head of the elementary school, agrees. "For us, the mission statement is the be-all and end-all. We refer to it all day long. Our alumni quote it. They love it and live it."

This climate of urgency and optimism in the face of tremendous odds is palpable throughout the school. This is not an accident, but an intended feature of a school culture founded by a civil rights activist determined to overcome the sad circumstances in which his families were caught. As the mission statement boldly proclaims, "We believe that we can change our conception of this world and our place within it."

With origins dating back to 1917, Providence St. Mel was a Catholic high school that resulted from the merger in 1968 of St. Mel and the Providence High School for Girls, which was founded in 1929. Ten years after the merger, during a further consolidation, the Archdiocese of Chicago announced that it was going to close the school. It was the last Catholic high school on the West Side.

Rather than let it close, Paul J. Adams III, the principal at the time and a participant in Dr. King's march from Selma to Montgomery, refounded it as an independent school. Soon afterward, bolstered by charitable donations drawn from around the country, he purchased the historic school property with the support of the General Superior of the Sisters of Providence.

Under Adams's leadership, the school expanded to serve the elementary grade levels while building its no-nonsense reputation as a school that had every one of its graduates accepted to college. Although Adams successfully passed the duties of school principal to Jeanette DiBella ten years ago, he remains the symbolic icon of the school, the president of the foundation that supports it, and the keeper of the school's climate and culture as a culture publicly committed to this larger mission.

"We're in the community, but not of the community," Adams remarks in his typical style that is one-part preacher and one-part prophet, but somehow so gentle it bears no hint of arrogance at all. "We want so much more for our students. This school is our effort to help them get that for themselves."

After thirty years of extraordinary success and a remarkable record of achievement that has changed forever the lives of the children who have gone through this school, Adams is clearly horrified that the plight of the innercity is actually worse today than when he started. But he remains more confident than ever that education is the great equalizer in society and that we need to dedicate ourselves more than ever to providing schools that are able to overcome the pathologies of the street—whatever they may be and however they may appear in the future.

"What's missing in inner-city education," Adams continues, "is the flexibility required to find out what works—to travel before you get there."

For anyone who has ever visited the school in person, this last comment may come as a big surprise. Innovation and

The Traditional Classroom Setting at PSM

flexibility are not the first words that come to mind when you think of Providence St. Mel. If anything, to the casual observer, the school gives off the distinct impression that it has been preserved in a time capsule for upward of fifty years. From the neo-Gothic school building that is immaculately maintained, with its slate chalkboards and built-in glass cabinetry that looks taken from a Victorian apothecary's shop, to the 2 × 2 square wood-framed windows that pull open above the classroom entranceways, the school exudes an air of old-world tradition that few other schools can touch. Throw in the traditional Catholic school classroom setup with wooden desks arranged in columns, the morning prayer and Pledge of Allegiance recited daily along with the mission statement over the PA, and second graders spelling out words on individual green chalk slates—and the overall picture is hardly cutting edge.

But to be left only with this impression is to miss Adams's point entirely.

Providence St. Mel is a highly disciplined school. The transitions in the hallways are quiet. Students keep their uniforms clean, and classroom instruction is delivered with few disturbances or any need to call on the school's behavior management system. A uniformed soldier responsible for the subtle pageantry of a presidential inauguration might emerge from a place like this. But none of this happens by magic. It happens because of hard work and a schoolwide attention to individual student needs.

"It's tough, but it's a tough *love* approach," says principal Jeanette DiBella, whose unrelenting focus on instructional practice and the specific needs of individual students has greatly accelerated overall student performance in recent years. "To succeed in this school, you have to be on task 90% to 95% of the time. If you are off task, we need to find out why. But the only way to do this effectively is to treat everyone with dignity and respect." Rather than disrupt class, students and teachers alike know to work with the school social worker to resolve specific issues that are keeping students from their classroom obligations. Marsha Spight, the school social worker, explains it this way: "There is a singular culture that we're promoting. But most children do not know how to do this on their own. They have to leave a lot behind to take success on board. The real task is to figure out what each one requires."

This is Paul Adams's point: "What's missing in inner-city education is the flexibility required to find out what works—to travel before you get there."

The long road that is traveled each day at Providence St. Mel is the hard road to meet each child, where she is—while holding up an ideal that everyone must strive to obtain.

It makes sense that DiBella is herself a specialist in emotional and behavioral disorders, not because these are the specific needs of the students in her school but because this training specifically directs one to consider the individual needs of students. Marci Van Gilder, professional development chair, makes this point perhaps as well as it can be made: "Students often have the hard work in their heart, but they've never had someone demand it of them. We'll work with them here until they get it. But it won't come out simply by demanding it. It is part of our culture to *know* the students and *respond* to them."

All across the school, in every individual classroom, you can see how this personalized level of attention makes Providence St. Mel what it is today. Positive, supportive, caring teachers at every turn praise what is done well and use what is partially correct to inspire the next level of achievement and understanding.

Eric Hendricks is teaching an AP Calculus class. Most likely, more than half of the students in the room were scoring below the twenty-fifth percentile in math when they came to Providence St. Mel. Today, he couldn't be more engaging, and they couldn't be more engaged. In mid-sentence, in the midst of solving an integral with the whole class contributing to the solution, this massive man bends down and stares one student in the eyes. "Put your finger on it. Tell us exactly where to go from here. I know you can do it. You can solve this for all of us." With one student now leading the way, the whole class is more engaged than ever.

In a third-grade language arts period, Antoine Jones is using an overhead projector to illustrate several different spellings of the long *O* sound. As she darts from student to student to check each response over their shoulders, somehow every child gets a private tutorial.

"Every day we say together, 'We will find a way or make one,'" Kevin McGrath quotes from the mission statement, as he takes out a practice exam for his life sciences students to consider.

"Well, how are we going to make it happen today?"

8

Arlington Traditional School

Arlington, Virginia

School Information	
855 N. Edison Street, Arlington, VA 22205 Phone: (703) 228-6290	Public Magnet 442 students Prekingergarten through Grade 5 59% white, 21% Asian, 12% Hispanic, 8% black

Cultural Traits Highlighted	Key Practices Featured
• A strong belief that culture determines outcomes	• Seven tenets of school's founding • Friday community assemblies
• A nurturing but demanding culture	• Fifth-grade safety patrol • Summer reading challenge
• A culture committed to student success	• Weekly summaries of student progress • Grade-level teaching teams
• A culture of people, principles, and purpose	• ABCs of Success

At the end of the day, quiet lines of school children file out of several different wings of the building, all converging at once on a single lobby and entrance way. At the foot of a large double-staircase stands Holly Hawthorne, the school's principal for sixteen years, and Donna Honeywell, her assistant principal for most all of that time. Together, they smile and wave. Occasionally, a few children break ranks to give one or both of them a spontaneous hug. From the top of the stairs, the quiet strains of music practice can be heard. It is likely a member of the fourth grade, all of whom study some musical instrument.

Down the hall, tiny little kindergarteners approach the lobby. Each is being held by the hand of a fifth grader wearing the neon yellow belt and silver badge of a crossing guard. Last week, the entire fifth-grade class was sworn in as the safety patrol and given their yellow belts to signify they are responsible for the safety of the entire school. Interspersed among the other students, members of the patrol calmly lead the lines of children outside to the front of the school where the buses await them to take them home. It is the tenth day of the school year.

Student Body and Faculty of Arlington Traditional School Assemble Outside of Main Entrance

ACADEMICS

The academic achievement that emerges from this environment is stunning. The quality of the first-grade writing posted in the hallways displays an understanding of complete sentence structure, capitalization, and punctuation—it could easily pass as solid third-grade work elsewhere. Although pass rates have ranged from 92.8% to 100% over the last five years, roughly 100% of the students here pass the Virginia Standards of Learning Assessment at all grades and in all subjects. Disadvantaged students who enter the school through the Virginia Preschool Initiative score at the highest levels, the fifth-grade history test is taken in fourth grade, and all of the fifth graders meet or exceed the state's eighth-grade technology expectations.

Arlington Traditional, or ATS as it is known locally, is a countywide alternative school that draws families attracted to its traditional philosophy from every neighborhood in Arlington. Although the school has increased in size to three classes per grade level and as recently as 2004 had a new addition completed—including the iconic main stairway and music rooms—the school has been at over capacity (up to 150%) for the last six years. Even though ATS has the largest kindergarten class size in all of Arlington, this fact does nothing to turn families away. Applications for kindergarten are received between February and April, and then students are selected for the following year by a random double-blind lottery. Only siblings and lower-income children who attended the school the year before through the Virginia Preschool Initiative are given automatic admission.[14] Today, the school serves 442 students in preK through fifth grade across a population as diverse as Arlington county itself, including more than 20% who speak one of fifteen foreign languages at home. There are waiting lists for admission into ATS at every grade level from every attendance zone in the district.

History of the School's Founding

Ironically, for all of its old-fashioned appeal, ATS was established by school board mandate as an alternative model to the educational experimentation then in vogue in the late 1970s. Most especially, ATS was a response to the open classrooms that dominated so many local public school districts at the time and the student-centered instructional methods they were supposed to help bring about.

In contrast to that approach, ATS has been guided by seven tenets since the school was founded in 1978:

- Teacher-guided instruction in self-contained classrooms
- Emphasis on basic education in the core academic areas
- Regular homework assigned to all grade levels
- Written weekly summary of student progress communicated to parents
- Promotion based on grade-level mastery
- Consistent behavior, dress, and grooming standards
- Weekly assembly programs reinforce philosophy and build community

In their simplicity, these tenets represent the core strength of the school and the seeds of its unique culture. In themselves, the tenets may not seem like much of a design statement, but over the years, through careful cultivation and an assiduous adherence to principle, the aspiration behind them has been infused into every detail of the school's daily activity.

The first five tenets are focused on academics; the sixth on the behavior that is expected of everyone; and the seventh on the character that is rewarded through the school's regular traditions, rites, and rituals. Everywhere in the school, these are referred to as the *ABCs of Success—Academics, Behavior, Character*. One thing you quickly realize about ATS is the school's gift for clear and consistent communication.

COMMUNICATION AND TRADITION

"We are very consistent with our message," Holly states simply. "You'll see it everywhere." She's not kidding. The ABCs of Success are literally everywhere in this school: on bulletin boards, on memos to parents, on bookmarks, on banners, on posters, and over doorways. But the ABCs of Success are *in* everything as well: in what they say and how they say it, in what they do at ATS, and how they choose to do it.

"You'll notice only two things in the hallway," Donna observes as we walk along, "positive messages and student work." Although many elementary schools work very hard to maintain colorful and inspirational bulletin boards along the school corridors, at ATS it is the celebration of student work that is unrelenting. Essays and presentations hang from every inch of the hallways punctuated only by reminders of the good behavior and sound character that underwrite the academics at the school. Curiously though, the whole affair is much more text heavy than you have seen anywhere else. It is words rather than pictures that spring from the walls. ATS has cultivated a conspicuously literary culture, and you begin to notice when you are there that you are always reading. Just after summer break, the only pictures on one hallway, in fact, are photographs or drawings of the students themselves mounted to certificates testifying to the number of pages that particular child read that summer. Every student at ATS, kindergartners included, pledges to read 50 books or 1,000 pages over the summer and practice their good character.[15] These certificates and the photos they contain prove that every student was true to their word. One girl managed to read more than 6,000 pages while on vacation.

If communication is a core virtue at ATS, then the simplicity, clarity, and consistency of the school's message is perhaps best displayed in action. "We have a lot of little traditions that people count on and then come to expect," Holly explains. "This is after all the Arlington *Traditional* School."

True to the school's founding tenets, the whole community assembles every Friday to wear the school colors and close the week on a high note by celebrating the learning and good works they have accomplished.

"Our colors are very dear to us," Holly says again with that signature simplicity for which ATS is known. "Blue stands for the blue ribbon—always do your best—and gold stands for the Golden Rule." On Friday, the whole school assembly is awash in blue and gold. At different times, they break into song or cheer and clap in recognition of various collective and individual accomplishments. One class performs a play of their devising to summarize what they have learned recently in science. The joy both in the giving and the receiving of the performance is palpable. The littlest students watch in awe. You begin to realize that you are seeing the ABCs of Success in action. However simple they may sound, they are a complete statement of what ATS aims to achieve—academics, behavior, and character. Before the students get ready to leave the assembly, they pull themselves together, stretch a bit, and quietly line up to head back to class. Holly concludes the assembly with the familiar words they hear each week, "Remember, take care of yourself and someone else."

ACCOUNTABILITY AND TEAMWORK

Of all the traditions, routines, and rituals that the school counts on and comes to expect, perhaps none is so well received as the weekly summaries.

Again, true to the school's founding tenets, each classroom teacher prepares an individual written summary of each student's weekly progress that both the student and their parents read, comment on, and sign. Each classroom can have a different format for these summaries, but they are all intended to address the academics, behavior, and character exhibited that week in class. Some teachers will include an overview of major whole-class activities or some announcements relevant to the entire group, but the primary purpose is to report and reflect on the achievement, work habits, and social development of each student over the last five days in school. "There is no doubt about it," Mr. Donald Martin says of his experience teaching in the fifth grade. "The weekly summary is one of the true powers of this school." The parents agree. "The communication in this school is phenomenal," one parent says who has children in the second and fourth grades. "With the weekly summary, there is accountability on both ends. Our children know what they did that week that they can improve on and what they need to do next week to be successful." Another parent goes further, "Nothing important gets lost in a week's time. Our children *buy into* what is expected of them because of the constant reminders. But they are able to *do* what is expected of them because of the constant support."

At the heart of this last observation is one of the school's greatest accomplishments. ATS has created a schoolwide culture that it fully expects will drive schoolwide outcomes, but in the end, it is individualized attention that drives so much individual student achievement. In the school culture as a whole, the structure that makes this possible is the combination of self-contained classrooms paired with extraordinary teamwork among grade-level teachers.

"Teacher-guided instruction in self-contained classrooms" is the primary tenet on which the school design was originally founded. While elementary school teachers all across the country still teach in self-contained classrooms, it is very rare today for one teacher to teach all subject areas without rotating in specialists of various kinds or rotating out the students to other classroom teachers. "Switching around classes dilutes your responsibility to the whole child," Mr. Martin states openly. "As a staff we end up talking about the children in detail to ensure they are successful. Instructionally, it is one of the pillars that makes this school great."

The point of view among the faculty at ATS, who on average have been at the school for more than ten years, is that the struggle to teach all the disciplines well within each self-contained classroom *requires* them to work well as a team and to learn from one another how best to tackle each subject and how best to address the specific needs of individual students. This is counterintuitive. One would think instructional interdependence, not self-contained classrooms, would lead to greater teamwork. The strong reply at ATS is that switching classrooms serves primarily to meet the needs of the teacher and takes the teacher's focus off the needs of the child. This is the distinction that makes all the difference.

"No class belongs to anyone—we're all responsible for all of the children," says Rex Goodwin, a third-grade teacher. "We *really* see each child as an individual student," Christine Mullins replies, "but no one person is *actually* able to do that well on their own." As if on cue, the kindergarten team leader, Mrs. Lorraine Gandy, adds, "If you have an *individual* student focus, you require a *team* approach." Again, this is the distinction that makes all the difference. It is deep within the school culture at ATS to serve the individual needs of each child, and to do that well, the faculty members have organized themselves into very strong, interdependent, grade-level teams. Their practice of teaching in self-contained classrooms could tempt them to shut the door and go it alone if it were not for the stronger cultural commitment to reporting on and being personally accountable to the parents for each child's progress every five school days.

School Improvement

Each of the school profiles featured in this book are intended to accomplish different things, but all of them aim to supply hope and direction: hope in what's possible in American schooling and direction for improving different aspects of a school's individual design. ATS is a particularly superb agent of both messages.

Of all the challenges that educators have to face throughout the year, it is often in the corporate attempt to "improve" a school that even worse problems are introduced. In an effort to improve literacy rates, for example, or increase the intensity of writing across the curriculum—a whole new curriculum is introduced, teachers have to be retrained on a massive scale, the existing planning time becomes insufficient to incorporate the new materials into proven lesson plans, the staff gets overworked, student achievement slides, morale drops, and leadership has to decide whether to stay the course and push harder on the required changes or to find a new path through the new problems at hand.

This is nothing unique to education. Change can often be painful, and where serious change management is required, things often get worse before they get better. That said, it is also true that school leaders—given how they are selected and assigned—often lack a basic vision for their particular school. Because of that, school leaders are also often susceptible to educational fads sold as panaceas and are even more susceptible to the education industry's monolithic acceptance of these fads as cure-alls worth taking. Whole language, open classrooms, heterogeneous groupings, homogeneous groupings—it does not matter—all of them require context to be made meaningful. If you don't know what you're washing, you make it easy to throw out the baby with the bathwater.

The story of ATS, on the other hand, demonstrates the power in one school's adherence to vision. ATS shows what great good can come of a consistent application of a coherent approach that is rigorously and regularly monitored for quality.

"We do everything by design—nothing here happens by chance," Donna states plainly, giving you some insight into the detailed planning required to achieve consistently outstanding results. "We're always backward planning from whatever result we're looking for—ideally you want teachers to use every minute available, and so you plan for every minute of the day."

Although time on the job and repetition can ease the over-all assignment implied by this kind of attention to detail (making Holly and Donna's job easier today than when they first teamed up ten years ago), nothing removes the instruc-tional leader's obligation to assess what is going well and what can be done better. For this reason, the faculty and administration go away on a retreat every year to reflect on their practice, discuss school improvement, and agree what will be done in the year ahead to help them achieve their schoolwide goals. I say to Holly that she makes it sound so easy. She replies, "It does *sound* easy: hire people who love kids, love teaching, and always want to improve themselves." And then she laughs, knowingly. What she knows is that if you make it sound easy—you actually make it easier for other people to achieve it.

ARLINGTON ACADEMY OF HOPE

There is perhaps no greater example of this last claim than the story of John Wanda and the founding of the Arlington Academy of Hope. John and his wife Joyce grew up in the villages of Bumwalukani and Bupoto in rural eastern Uganda. After immigrating to the United States in June 1996 and settling in Arlington, Virginia (by way of a diversity visa from the U.S. State Department), they were so moved by their children's education at ATS that they worked to provide a similar opportunity for the children in their native land.

After first, being unsatisfied by the impact they could have providing scholarship money for the children back home, they decided instead to open a village school and model it after ATS complete with the ABCs of Success and the summer reading challenge. Since February 2004, the Arlington Academy of Hope (AAH) is the only school in the region that, according to its founders, "uses American models of education, serves lunch, and emphasizes the development of the child as an individual" (Arlington Academy of Hope, 2010, para. 4). Now in its sixth year of operation, the school is far and away the highest performing among almost 150 government schools in the district of Bududa. Last year, 97% of the students scored in the top two of four divisions on the national exams and AAH sent 100% of its first two graduating classes onto secondary school as compared to a more typical 14% matriculation rate (Arlington Academy of Hope, 2010). All throughout the school back in Arlington, Virginia, there are colorful reminders of their sister school on the African continent. Holly's office is covered in photographs of her and other faculty members' visits to Uganda for teacher training. Bulletin boards along the hallway proudly display the letters ATS and AAH—"We come from all over Arlington and all over the world."

Students at ATS and AAH Celebrate Their Sister School a Continent Away

Simply having a conversation with the students at ATS proves the proposition that if you cultivate the environment, it will create the outcomes. Anytime you wish, the children will eagerly talk to you (and always with their signature poise and cheerfulness) of what they know about their pen pals over the ocean and what their school has done to bring such extraordinary opportunity to others. Holly attributes this again to the clarity and focus of the school's message. "The ABCs enable us to talk to everyone in easy to understand language that transcends any differences," she explains. The experience of being at the school, however, is more profound than she makes it sound. You can't help but think an entire community heard in the back of its mind, "Take care of yourself and someone else," and, at the same time, had the skills, the motivation, and the willingness to pull it off.

9

HOPE Prima

Milwaukee, Wisconsin

School Information	
2345 N. 25th Street Milwaukee, WI 53206 Phone: (414) 931–0350 Fax: (414) 931–0702	Private 220 students Prekindergarten through Grade 8 99.5% black

Cultural Traits Highlighted	Key Practices Featured
• A strong belief that culture determines outcomes	• Community of faith, hope, and love • Weekly chapel assemblies
• A nurturing but demanding culture	• Positive approach to student discipline
• A culture committed to student success	• HYSTEP: hello, yes, smile, thank you, excuse me, and please
• A culture of people, principles, and purpose	• Professional culture among staff

For more than two decades now, the city of Milwaukee has been ground zero in the national struggle over school choice. Wherever in the country advocates have fought to provide direct purchasing power over education to parents, the voice and experience of the Milwaukee Parental Choice Program has always been front and center. Implemented in 1990 as the nation's first private school voucher program, today more than 100 schools and 20,000 students are enrolled in the program.[16]

HOPE Prima, the oldest of the three HOPE Christian Schools, is a school of choice. As a private school, it has freedoms that other schools in this book are not at liberty to enjoy, but the school also chooses to serve a very different need. By design, it is a response to those most in need. As Andrew Neumann, the president of the school system puts it, "We intentionally setup our schools in underserved neighborhoods because we believe that every child has the capacity to learn, but not every child is given that opportunity."

Founded in 2002, HOPE Prima serves 220 children in kindergarten through eighth grade of whom 96% are eligible for free lunch, 99.5% are black, and 98.6% participate in the Milwaukee Parental Choice Program (MPCP). The HOPE schools are affiliated with the Lutheran Church. HOPE's network of three schools serve 20% of MPCP students enrolled at Lutheran schools and about 4% of all students in the program.

The very real need for a different kind of school comes through loud and clear from the parents who have made the choice to send their children to HOPE.

Charmaine Gee and Sherice Jones both went to Milwaukee public schools and, for a number of years, sent their children to local schools in the system. Recently, they became frightened by the rate of change they witnessed in the school community and the poor quality of schooling they were expected to tolerate. "I just got fed up with the lack of relationship between my children and their teachers," Sherice says. Charmaine then adds, "It's terrible how quickly that environment can pull you down. You have to reprogram your child at the end of every day." Unwilling to take it any longer, Sherice now has all of her children ages four, seven, eight, thirteen, and fourteen either enrolled or in line to go to HOPE. Charmaine also has her children enrolled at HOPE Prima. They are seven and thirteen.

Families that want greater continuity between what is learned at home and what is taught in school (and families that for whatever reason cannot provide much structure at home) take great comfort in how seriously the concepts of team and family are brought to life every day through the school culture at HOPE.

Students Transition to Class in a Hallway at HOPE Prima

Upon walking through the front door, you can see a lot of similarities with the very best schools all across the country serving low-income inner-city youth. You see the university pennants and the other tangible signs intended to make college aspirations real; the data clearly displayed on walls showing regular progress toward bold academic goals; and the constant reminders that what the students are doing is hard work, so they'll have to work hard to achieve it. The banners read no limits, no excuses.

Over the last ten years, many school leaders inspired by visits to KIPP (The Knowledge Is Power Program founded by Michael Feinberg and David Levin now operating ninety-nine schools in twenty states and the District of Columbia) and other No Excuses Schools have created high-performing school cultures of their own after much the same model.[17] Unwilling to let innocent school children be consumed by the sad legacies of poverty, racism, and broken homes that hold back so many schools in the inner city, these school leaders answered the calling of their time and created high-quality public schools to serve those largely abandoned by the establishment. Out of this effort came dozens of school networks and hundreds of schools all powered by great teaching and held together by school cultures committed to meeting the individual needs of low-income children. And then there is HOPE.

Often called "the Christian KIPP" by those who see the similarities on the surface, HOPE is so much more. Yes, the students roll their multiplication tables and sing other dynamic chants to get their hearts, heads, and hands in sync—"*Have you ever seen a scholar as smart as me?*" But the school's choral chant, "We are HOPE, HOPE!" that often morphs more into a battle cry, "We are HOPE, HOPE!" comes from a deeper place and calls on a deeper reality to make the school what it is today.

On the wall is a banner that you will not see in 90% of America's schools. It reads,

I can do all things through Christ who gives me strength.

—Philippians 4:13

Properly understood as a Christ-centered school, HOPE's mission to inspire, equip, and support serving leaders to transform the world around them is not just different in degree from the many schools whose practices it may imitate; it is different in kind.

The community at HOPE is first and foremost a community of faith. As an article of that faith, students and teachers

A Group of First Graders Listen Attentively During Chapel Service

at HOPE are brought together in community through the person of Christ. This is not a symbolic bond, but an essential union they share with one another as sons and daughters of God with the same hope for the future and sharing the same eternal purpose. It is the depth of this bond that enables HOPE to achieve its mission.

In secular traditions, it is often said there are four virtues on which the door of the moral life hinges: (1) fortitude, (2) temperance, (3) prudence, and (4) justice. In the Christian tradition, added to these four cardinal virtues were three theological virtues of (1) faith, (2) hope, and (3) love with the greatest of these being love. They are called "theological" because God is both the proper object of the virtuous habit and the ultimate source of the virtue as well. For the Christian, the ability to love anyone or anything is thus a participation in the life of God who is Love alone.

Many great school leadership teams across the country freely use the word *love* throughout the school day, but when describing their work to outsiders, they sometimes talk as if the word is somehow forbidden. At HOPE, the word *love* is used with vigor.

"An environment where love, laughter, and learning can flourish is essential," says Jamie Luehring, the school's principal. "As any family should, we strive to treat one another with respect, communicate openly and often, and *cherish the intrinsic value each of us possesses as individuals.*" According to Luehring, the concept of love understood in its deepest sense supercharges the entire teaching enterprise to be fundamentally about realizing human value. Whether or not a school has a religious orientation, there is a truth operating at the center of this observation that all teachers can benefit from.

"When teachers are not driven by love," Luehring says with a wry smile, "achieving success with student behavior and academics is more difficult—and there are easier ways to make a living." The truth lived at HOPE is that teaching is not a job—but a calling. The motivation to love your students and so to serve them in love is not an instructional technique but a response to a deep and abiding belief that the intrinsic value of the child demands no less than God's love for that child from the teacher. "Our faith in God is what keeps us going," Luehring concludes by saying, "and our belief that God is doing this work—transfers to them." It is at the intersection of this belief and the different kind of teaching it inspires that the miracles happen.

"They love us," one eighth-grade student says of the entire faculty. "They don't have to do this," another girl asserts. "And they wouldn't if they didn't love us," the first girl concludes with a certainty that sounds like it comes from experience.

Is that why you are a student at HOPE, I want to ask. Do you come here because the teachers are different? How does it compare to the school you came from? And have you changed as a student here in any way?

"There is no comparison," one cheerful boy replies with a smile as big as Christmas morning on his face. "What we *want* is different," he says, smiling. "We can't just do what we *want* to. We have to *want* what we're doing here." Suddenly, a whole group of students begins to nod their heads as if they too were spoken for. HOPE really is a different kind of school, they explain. And they are different people as a result.

"A love for teaching is not only encouraged it's required at HOPE." Liz Hochtritt, the seventh- and eighth-grade math teacher, says during a separate conversation with a number of teachers, "But higher Terra Nova scores are not going to get them to heaven." With that one statement, it becomes clear that the teachers are consciously trying to do something different in their classrooms at HOPE. "We are all trying to model and reflect Christ's love," second-grade teacher Lindsey Gerke adds simply—and the whole room goes comfortably quiet— as if nothing more need be added.

Many great school leaders and their leadership teams speak of the importance of shared vision when it comes to creating and sustaining a coherent school culture. It is only in "seeing" the same thing—in having a shared vision of an ideal not yet realized—that a team of disparate individuals can work together in concert to build a place of unified purpose where the whole is greater than the collection of their individual efforts. But that is not the lesson to be taken from HOPE. More important than the shared vision is the shared reality: What they believe the truth to be is the same, and it is a truth that both makes demands on them and allows them to be demanding of others.

It is the same truth that allows the staff and administration at HOPE to speak so freely of their love that also allows them to speak freely of what that love requires. This is the edge that HOPE has on so many schools that aspire to serve children with the greatest needs. Their real faith and hope in God allows them to love openly and to be open to the tremendous sacrifices that love enjoins.

"You really need to *believe* you can get it done," Jamie Luehring says, reflecting on the trials of his first year at the school. "I hit rock bottom and broke down. But then I realized that if we can't do this, nobody can. And I really believed that. Once I really believed that, serious change started happening."

It is because the staff and administration are so confident in Christ's unconditional love for them that they so freely give of themselves to their students and their colleagues. At the same time, it is their shared understanding that they alone are insufficient to meet this task that tempers those disagreements that always arise in the face of challenging work. "It is easy to get negative when things get hard," Luehring continues. "You need to talk to each other and have the tough conversations. We still struggle, we still fight like family, but we love each other when we walk away."

This confidence of a school community to truly love one another like family members—who also because of that love make real demands on one another—perhaps reaches a higher expression in religious settings. That said, maybe the greatest lesson coming out of HOPE is that the willingness to love is also a habit that a community can learn and cultivate.

We have heard how the children at HOPE feel loved. This is not just the by-product of a Christian community's faith in God shared with their students; this is the intentional result of very purposeful human action. The environment is as friendly as any you have ever entered. The building is warm, brightly lit, and spotless. By design, the instructional staff members ensure that they make five positive comments for every one that disciplines. You hear many more children thanked publicly for their good behavior than ever you hear students called in to line. Genuine Midwestern manners are proudly in evidence: Even the youngest kindergartners eagerly hold the door open for you. In fact, every classroom has posters reminding students to HYSTEP it, that is, say hello, yes, smile, thank you, excuse me, and please.

In the midst of this mild-mannered and genuinely polite society, there is a palpable sense of the human dignity that is being cultivated alongside it. At the weekly chapel assembly, after awards have been given to individual students for various academic accomplishments, grand silken banners that would look at home on a military parade ground are awarded to those grade levels in a schoolwide competition that produced the best attendance and homework completion rates that week. This week, the sixth-grade class captured the homework banner for 99% of all assignments complete. At this same assembly, red and blue, silver and blue, and finally gold and blue ties are awarded to those students who have earned the highest honors. At the start of the school year, all students wear the same solid blue ties. "Culture building is a work in progress," points out Krysta DeBoer, who teaches seventh- and eighth-grade English language arts. "Every year we add more things. New students now have to earn their ties to show they've kept the covenant."

And the effect of these details is apparent on the students. "Our ties stand for team and family," one boy explains. "We're proud of them because we've worked for them."

Again, the students are a positive reflection of the environment established by their teachers, and their tone is an imitation of what is modeled before them. When so many male faculty members at even the best schools these days struggle to find a necktie that coordinates with their flannel shirt, you notice the well-pressed suits, the clean-cut look, and the wholesome appearance of the entire HOPE staff. Taken altogether, the combined effect is more formal than you typically find even at elite private schools, but given the modesty of the staff and the manner in which they so sincerely personalize what they say—the overall impression given is one of a very *professional* organization. "We take pride in our team's professionalism," says Andrew Neumann, the president of the school network. But this pride certainly is not limited to their personal decorum and appearance, "We encourage and reward innovative thinking and high performance."

Hidden in this last comment are two important lessons that HOPE contributes to the understanding of how school culture is formed: (1) It can be done relatively quickly (2) if it is done with an eye to sustainability.

"In order to maintain a strong school you have to focus on a viable and sustainable teaching career," Neumann observes. Implied in this remark is the simple truth that so many of the other strong schools serving the inner city these days are doing so at a great personal price to their teachers who then leave the profession after two years for having to work unsustainably long hours to get the desired results. "We're all looking to increase time on task, but the 'on task' part is what matters." Luehring concludes by saying, "You want efficiency in your use of time so your staff stays fresh." To this end, Neumann openly encourages proactive problem solving and intelligent risk taking across the HOPE network while knowing that it is the only way they will identify sustainable approaches to serving these children, who require a great deal of attention but whom will not be well served by their teachers burning out. "This is a people business focused on individual students," Neumann adds. "To do that, you have to create an environment that attracts and keeps people. You need dynamic resilience."

The meaning of this last remark can best be seen in how HOPE's school culture really came to flourish out of the leadership restructuring that was put in place three years ago.

To make Luehring's job as the school principal more sustainable, HOPE added a director of operations position to oversee all school-level business affairs, the budget, the busing, and of course the school choice forms, which represent the largest source of the school's revenue. In addition, HOPE added a dean of students so that attention could be better given to individual student needs without taking Luehring's eye off the quality of instruction and, most especially, the needs of teachers.

Out of these improvements came other structural changes to help further embed the school culture and make the delivery of quality instruction more sustainable for everyone. "It's hard to get a new teacher up to speed in this building," Luehring remarks of the support required to properly orient anyone to the details of a well-designed and intentional environment. As a solution, new teachers serve as teaching assistants for the first year on the job, as funding allows, and there is an open-door policy in all classrooms so that the entire teaching staff can learn from one another throughout the year. "I think we're now at the point where we can grow because we've built the strong foundation," Luehring says confidently.

And growth is in the works for the HOPE schools because of the extraordinary demand for their offering. The schools continue to reach out to families, some 44% of whom do not have high school diplomas themselves. Their children arrive at HOPE testing two or more years below grade level, but after five to six years, they see a national percentile ranking increase of twenty-five to fifty points. But growth is also in the works for the HOPE schools because they know how much more they can improve. Over the last three years, the percentage of students testing out of the bottom quartile on the Star math exam has improved 52% while the percentage of students who are now in the top two quartiles has increased

Students in Prayer Before Class Begins

51%. But with 63% percent of the student body advanced or proficient in math, that still leaves an awfully important 37% percent that require even more focused time and attention.

But growth is most certainly in the works for the HOPE schools because of the nature of their mission to form servant leaders after the model of Jesus Christ who came not to save a few but all mankind. It reminds one of another scriptural quotation you see on the walls and from which the school gets its name. It reads,

In His name the nations will put their hope.

—Matthew 12:21

10

Cotswold Elementary

Charlotte, North Carolina

School Information	
300 Greenwich Road Charlotte, NC 28211 Phone: (980) 343 6720 Fax: (980) 343–6739	Public Magnet 499 students Kindergarten through Grade 5 45% white, 43% black, 11% Hispanic

Cultural Traits Highlighted	Key Practices Featured
• A strong belief that culture determines outcomes	• International Baccalaureate
• A nurturing but demanding culture	• Teaching through inquiry and reflection
• A culture committed to student success	• Day books drive assessment for learning
• A culture of people, principles, and purpose	• Shared schoolwide commitment to character formation

"**N**o one asks you what SAT scores you got after you make it into college," says Bonnie Henry, the speech therapist at Cotswold. "But who you are as a person stays with you always. This is the most important thing a child can learn in school. We need to help them decide who they want to become and how they want to live their lives."

Cotswold Elementary is ten minutes from the NASCAR Plaza smack in the center of Charlotte, North Carolina. A modern-day boomtown, Charlotte's population has grown by nearly a third in the last ten years. Following on the extraordinary success of the motor-raceway enterprise, the growth of U.S. Airways with its principle hub in Charlotte, and all the financial business that now makes the city the second-largest banking center in the country, people are flocking to this southeastern metropolis looking for new opportunity and a renewed quality of life.

Ceramic Tiles Created by Fourth Graders at Cotswold Celebrate State Symbols Dear to North Carolina

Charlotte-Mecklenburg, as a school district, made national news under the leadership of Eric Smith, the famed superintendent who from 1996 to 2002 worked to turn the district around through a relentless focus on high-level performance metrics that he then drove through the system to elevate the math and reading scores of all schools, but most especially the lowest performing schools serving the most disadvantaged youth. It was at this same time that the district's thirty-year-old court-ordered busing ruling came to an end resulting in a huge influx of low-performing children into Cotswold, who previously had been bused to suburban schools for integration purposes but who had been neglected while there.

According to many parents who were there at the time, the suspension of the busing rules combined with a redrawing of what neighborhoods Cotswold would draw from nearly destroyed the school. Families left in droves. Faced now with a raucous, sometimes unruly, but genuinely undereducated new population of children, the school realized that it had to do something different.

Trained in the methods made popular by Phil Vincent, the faculty made an explicit schoolwide commitment to use literature as the basis for the character formation of their students. Bonnie Henry helped to lead the effort securing the grant funds for the training while working with her colleagues to see the many benefits of addressing their needs in this way. "Children are going to read," Henry says simply. "Make sure they read something worthy and that their reading imparts the life lessons they need to be successful—not just in school, but in life—what they need to know to be happy."

If children do not know how to share, they should read about and discuss the value of sharing in class. Children need to read about and discuss with one another in their own words what it means to be courageous, generous, prudent, and fair. Children need to read about, through great examples in literature, and learn for themselves, in discussion with their peers and with adults whom they trust, what is most valuable in life and how they can make that their own.

According to Bonnie Henry, even the most hardened teachers in the school at the time thought the training and the commitment to character formation through literature was the most important turning point in their professional careers. The parents noticed as well. "We tell our children where and when you are born are matters of luck," one father says. "But we chose to send our children to Cotswold over the best private schools in the area because what they learn here is what makes a person successful in life."

At the center of a major metropolitan area currently in a growth phase, the local neighborhood surrounding Cotswold is a naturally diverse community with Russian immigrants, Muslim Africans, as well as lower-, middle-, and upper-middle-class whites living alongside one another in a regularly changing cosmopolitan landscape. As one parent, Kathy Gibbs, memorably puts it, "Wonderfully for this school, we don't have to force integration through busing because it occurs here naturally."

When Eric Smith eventually left Charlotte for Anne Arundel County, Maryland, he took Donna Cianfrani with him, who had been the principal of Cotswold from 1997, and helped make the school's brand of character formation and student discipline a district model to follow. Denise Hearne has been in the principal's chair since then, bringing increased academic rigor to the school while developing further the warm and caring culture that has made Cotswold such a local treasure to cherish.

"How do you raise test scores has become *the* conversation," Hearne remarks about the challenges of being a school leader in the era after No Child Left Behind. "It has to be a critical part of our work, but you'll lose focus on the children if they become a score."

The tension inherent in this last remark is particularly telling coming from Hearne because Cotswold is a school now whose culture as a very welcoming and child-centered environment is so obvious that it has a certain aura about it, yet this last year failed to make adequately yearly progress (AYP) in

Diverse Student Body Stands in Front of the Attributes of the
International Baccalaureate Learner Profile

certain subgroups.[18] Part of the solution for Cotswold under
Hearne's direction has been to make the school an International
Baccalaureate (IB) magnet and use the framework of the IB
Primary Years Program to focus the faculty as needed to
strengthen the instruction and drive achievement where previ-
ously some students may have been underserved.

"Now that we're embracing the IB concept, you'll see
more of the academic piece come forward," Hearne summarizes. "Cotswold has long understood what is required to
make students happy, but to be successful in a demanding
world of all kinds of people requires additional skills. IB is just
expanding our vision of what students really need to know
and what academic success really means."

This comment is instructive for at least two reasons: (1) It
suggests that the real academic success that Cotswold desires is

something *broader* than what Cotswold was pursuing earlier—even though one major challenge on hand (rather narrowly focused) is the test scores of certain students, and (2) it explicitly says that the sequence of building a school culture starts with student happiness and then moves to other outcomes.

You hear this implied sequence of culture building across all constituencies at Cotswold. The parents, teachers, and even the students themselves are aware that the school is a work in progress, but they are "more aware" in some way that they are building their school culture first around the character of their students and then will more directly pursue what those students need to be competitive in today's world.

Mary Hooks spent five years teaching in the gifted program at Cotswold before becoming the schoolwide IB facilitator. "Because the school has successfully changed to become a school of character, we were able to use that to become better educators and add more rigor," Hooks explains. Bonnie Henry draws this observation out further: "Program integration and people integration are key to any successful school environment, but you first need a *respectful staff* to integrate anything."

There is quite a lot of teaching embedded in these last few comments: For schools to be great, they have to be schools of character first. But schools of character require that the faculty are people of character themselves, able to work well with others in service to a greater good—a shared schoolwide vision of individual student success.

Denise Hearne's individual career appears to have prepared her well for the assignment at hand. She started in education as a teacher for eleven years working with children with behavioral and emotional disabilities. "That training immediately gets you to see students *individually*," she comments with absolute emphasis. "That is where the difference lies—you have to really learn to listen to children and get them to find their voice. No two kids are exactly alike, and it is precisely the similarities among students that requires an individual focus to draw them out."

After a short stint in district administration, which she decidedly did not like, she became a district-level teacher observer and professional developer. Not only did this give her broad experience refining the instructional techniques of others, but her work was carried out during the era of outcomes-based education, and she was regularly put in the awkward position of answering the question, "If there's a specific *outcome* intended—whose *values* are you teaching?"

"The only way to answer that question," Hearne comments dryly, "is to ask what do parents want for their children. In my experience, the answer is to be happy and productive—those are the outcomes we are seeking."

As for whose values are being taught now at Cotswold, one of the great strengths of the IB program is its method of teaching through inquiry and reflection. Although the IB learner profile, as an ideal statement of learning outcomes, articulates ten traits that the program looks to see in its students, these traits and the students' expression of them are mostly discovered and then made one's own through study.[19] In other words, the IB program does not present a values system that is imposed on the school. Rather, by embracing the IB framework, the school creates the opportunity for its students to discern for themselves a coherent system of values that they can take into the world on their terms.

If this is beginning to sound a lot like Cotswold's original "commitment to character formation through literature" taken to the next level, then the pattern is becoming clear.

"IB teaches children how to learn, how to inquire, and how to reflect more deeply on what they learn," Hearne explains. "These are the skills they will need to know to adapt to this changing world." Hearne then takes her observation to the next level, citing the fantastic rate at which subject knowledge is being rendered obsolete—leaving knowledge acquisition and interpersonal communications as the key skills all people will need in the age to come: "We can't prepare them in any other way for the future because the world they will participate in does not exist yet."

If inquiry is the primary method of teaching now at Cotswold, reflection is what makes it stick. From kindergarten on up, students keep day books or personal accounts of their developing experiences in school. Through them, students keep a running log of what they have learned and what that learning has meant to them. But they are also encouraged to take responsibility for their personal growth and development and so students at Cotswold reflect on their behavior in the day books and tie their individual actions to larger accomplishments or disappointments they encounter along the way. "Reflecting on what went wrong in a day is like shooting foul shots in basketball," the precociously named Michael Shepard-Moore told me while reviewing his day book. "If you go left, you need to find out what will bring it to the right. Sometimes you can learn more from setbacks." Portfolios of student work—which also include personal reflections on their progress to date—provide a written record of students analyzing their work, setting future goals, and developing action plans to improve their progress.

It quickly becomes apparent why IB is such a good fit for Cotswold at this stage in its growth and why the previously accomplished schoolwide commitment to character formation helped the IB program take root so quickly.

As an instructional tool, daily access to individual student reflection on their learning—as is collected in the day books— is the best possible source of information an educator could want who is looking to identify individual student needs and fine-tune instruction accordingly. At the same time, if students are not motivated to take responsibility for their learning and to be responsible citizens in a larger community of learners, it is unlikely that the exercise of keeping day books would last long in practice or yield much real fruit to improve that practice further. A school that is committed to character first can more easily strive to be a high-performing school next.

Kailey was highly dyslexic. In third grade, her parents took her out of a local Christian school, and she was placed in a bimodal second/third grade at Cotswold. Now, she is scoring in the ninety-eighth percentile on the state accountability exam known as the End-of-Grade test in North Carolina and, recently, won a local science fair for her presentation on energy conservation.

Yusef Osman is a Bantu of Somalia and one of six children raised in Kenyan refugee camps before being relocated to the United States through a Catholic social services resettlement program. When he first came to Cotswold, he was identified by Bonnie Henry and the other specialists in the building as low functioning. He is now in the gifted program. He has made all As and Bs on his report card (with the exception of one C) for the past two years. "Teachers find the way we'll learn—whatever it is," Yusef explains modestly, while the other children around the room smile for him.

And what do you learn from one another in this school? I ask, wanting to know more about the diverse environment and the international character of the IB program. "One thing I absolutely love about this school is the hearing impaired students," a fifth grader, Luci Gates, blurts out enthusiastically and with no fear of making a non sequitur. "Although there are differences between us, they aren't differences that divide us—they are differences we can learn from."

The parents of these children are now evangelists for a school they cannot believe they have access to or are so lucky to have in their backyard—for 71% of them, Cotswold is their local school while the other 29% come in through the magnet program. "It's a community where everyone supports one another," says Cathy Chick, a Charlotte native of more than thirty years whose family came in through the magnet program. "What is so impressive to me is how the children naturally care for one another and how willing they are to help each other learn as a result."

D. C. Lucchesi went to a Christian Brothers school in Memphis. "We are getting here what I thought we could only get from a Catholic school. The kids don't just get a focused education; they get seven to eight hours a day of who and what they want to be."

Although some may be uncomfortable with parents of public school students citing the moral formation of religious denominations as something they want out of their local school, the parents in this group are quite at home with the conversation. Tim Moore is a Baptist pastor and the father of triplets who also selected Cotswold over a highly rated private school in his neighborhood. Because the triplets have been placed in separate classrooms as they have gone through Cotswold, he has interacted with nearly every teacher on the faculty and can attest to their personal commitment to the children and how that trusting relationship helps drive learning. "This has nothing to do with religion," he declares. "This is simply sound education. This is the kind of moral formation that children need for the twenty-first century."

11

Atlantis Elementary

Port St. John, Florida

School Information	
7300 Briggs Avenue Port St. John, FL 32927 Phone: (321) 633–6143 Fax: (321) 633–6038	Public 720 students Kindergarten through Grade 6 81% white, 7% multiracial, 6% black, 5% Hispanic
Cultural Traits Highlighted	**Key Practices Featured**

• A strong belief that culture determines outcomes	• Six core virtues:
	  (1) trustworthiness
	  (2) respect
	  (3) responsibility
	  (4) fairness
	  (5) caring
	  (6) citizenship
	• Class-level vision statements

• A nurturing but demanding culture	• Rachel's Challenge • Psychological safety among faculty to take risks and challenge one another
• A culture committed to student success	• Highly individualized instruction • Classroom-level rules • Grade-level team planning time

When Yuri Gagarin, the famed Soviet cosmonaut, returned safely to Earth after the very first manned mission to outer space, the people of the United States were at once thrilled by the human accomplishment and horrified by the prospect of the Red Terror's further dominance in the space race. President Kennedy, determined to motivate this country with an audacious goal, framed his positive message with the following words:

> I believe that this nation should commit itself to achieving the goal, before this decade is out, of landing a man on the Moon and returning him safely to the Earth. No single space project in this period will be more impressive to mankind, or more important in the long-range exploration of space; and none will be so difficult or expensive to accomplish. (Kennedy, 1961)

Among all human endeavors, manned spaceflight remains among the boldest expressions of innovation and engineering ever attempted. But without the raw courage to *man* the mission, all the technological advancement and ingenuity would be to no avail. Without the hope to learn of greater things beyond, the tenacity to withstand unspeakable trials, and the perseverance to strive in the face of the most unlikely odds— there never would have been a start to the Apollo space program, let alone the extraordinary record of achievement that landed twelve men on a remote celestial body and returned them safely to Earth. Again, as President Kennedy, in a different speech, presented the purpose of the Apollo program and the virtues required to get the work done:

> We choose to go to the moon in this decade and do the other things, not because they are easy, but because they are hard, because that goal will serve to organize and measure the best of our energies and skills, because that challenge is one that we are willing to accept, one we are unwilling to postpone, and one which we intend to win. (Kennedy, 1962)

Titusville, Florida, and the adjoining towns of Cocoa Beach and Port St. John did not become household names in the 1960s like Cape Canaveral, but together, they are home to the men and women who power this portion of the U.S. space program. True to the ethic of those who live here, Titusville is known as "A City of Service." In addition to the National Police Museum, with its mission to care for the families and children of officers killed in the line of duty, this area is world renowned for a swath of land just over the Indian River drawbridge and the long causeway that separates the mainland from the Merritt Island wildlife preserve: the John F. Kennedy Space Center.

Three elementary schools in Port St. John—Atlantis, Enterprise, and Challenger 7—all named for space shuttles which would continue the heyday of manned missions to outer space after the Apollo program, feed into a singular regional middle school and another senior high school that serve the space coast.[20] Atlantis mostly draws from the front of the area, which is a combination of renters and some more established families, but with the recent changes that the school is seeing in shifting demographics and families moving in with one another, the 45% of students who qualify for the federal lunch program is likely to be an underreported number.

The overall picture could be of many places in America. The school is somewhat hidden from view, tucked away in a neighborhood among small low-lying ranch houses of a stucco finish. Palm trees and other thickset plantings punctuate small but carefully manicured lawns. Clearly in evidence are the disciplined habits of hardworking people of modest incomes. As of the 2000 census, the median income for households in the area was $44,030 (U.S. Census Bureau, 2000).

Sticking with the space coast theme, the sign outside the school says, "Atlantis Elementary: Launching the Future." But a much greater impression is made by eight huge columns in the central courtyard labeled in large block letters, "Kids for character—trustworthiness, respect, responsibility, fairness, caring, and citizenship." These six virtues are those incorporated into the Character Counts! program

Pillars in Central Courtyard at Atlantis Name the Six Character
Traits

developed by the Josephson Institute, an organization
founded in 1987 to increase ethical commitment in all seg-
ments of society. More than any other character rubric uncov-
ered during the research for this book, this framework was
seen the most often. According to the organization, it is the
largest character program in the country (The Josephson
Institute, 2010). Without rehearsing here the relative merits of
these virtues taken together as a set, it is important to observe
that they are most vibrant where they have long been incorporated into the life of the school. True to this pattern,
Atlantis has long been a school intentionally working on its
culture and the effect of that culture on the character of its
students. In 1999, in the second year that the Character
Education Partnership awarded the national school of character award, Atlantis Elementary won.

   In this context, Sherry Tomlinson and Vanessa Judson
have inherited a school culture that is theirs not only to

continue but also to adapt to the future with all its unknown challenges. Tomlinson spent her first five years in education as a teacher at Atlantis. After a career teaching and serving as an administrator throughout Brevard County, Tomlinson returned seven years ago to take the helm as principal. Under Tomlinson's leadership, Atlantis Elementary has received the Florida Power Media award, the Brevard Cultural Alliance Excellence in Visual Arts award, had four teachers recognized as Exemplary Science Teachers by the Space Coast Science Education Alliance, and was awarded the Brevard County Teacher of the Year for both 2006–2007 and 2009–2010 school years.

"When I came to Atlantis, I thought it was all about data," Tomlinson remarks of her return to the school. "We're still deeply data-driven, but the relationships are prior to everything else." Spending anytime at all with Tomlinson and her team makes the real meaning of this last remark more obvious. While strolling around the school under a covered walkway that connects the classrooms to one another, Tomlinson picks up stray pieces of trash like so many other principals who personally care for the environment entrusted to them, but you can see in her eyes that she is looking for individual children. She is not waiting to see whom she runs into or what conversations emerge along the way; she is looking out for specific students who are on her mind.

"Wait here," she says, "I'll be right back." With no notice, she leaves the walkway and bounds onto the playing fields that border that side of the school. With little care for her heeled shoes or the hems of her black suit pants, she nimbly jogs across the damp field to get to the other side of a PE class racing through an obstacle course that morning. She leans down to talk to a single child with autism who had been out of school for several days. After a brief conversation and a warm hug, she walks away smiling, waving to all the other children in line who are getting ready to run through a row of tires like so many star running backs. Over the next several hours, while walking through the school, she'll manage to personally check on every single student who had been out of school recently for one reason or another.

"It's all about relationships," Tomlinson says again. "You get success when kids know that somebody cares about them and believes they can be successful."

The personal relationships with the children at Atlantis are only matched by the high regard with which the faculty and administration approach one another and respect one another's professional capabilities. Both Tomlinson and Judson clearly are teachers first and relish their hands-on connection with the details of instruction and how that brings them closer in contact with their colleagues and the students.

For this reason, the quality, variety, and level of personalization brought to the instruction at Atlantis are astounding. What at first appears to be a second-grade lesson (delivered as whole-class instruction) is actually a highly differentiated exercise with each student learning to take notes and summarize the steps of a process according to very different ability levels. In a fifth-grade shared-pair discussion, students help one another go deeper in their understanding of the essay form from topic sentence through supporting details to conclusion. In a sixth-grade science class, all at once, small-group discussions cover Newton's laws of motion, how to qualify field observations, and various methods of testing a hypothesis. "We work very hard to encourage each other to reflect each day on what can be done better or done differently," Judson notes.

In the midst of all this attention given to the art and mechanics of teaching, what appears to be even more artfully crafted and more consistently enforced is the overall environment in which student learning takes place. Atlantis is a morally charged environment deep in expressions of each citizen's obligations to self and others.

As but one example, each grade level composes a vision statement of how it sees itself, how it wants to be seen, and ultimately, what it wants to become. Most classes in each grade then adapt this statement into a more particular class-level vision. Many of the classrooms at Atlantis then further develop their own class rules which they agree to enforce for one another's benefit and which the students then contractually sign and post in their classrooms.

"What we do is not a program of any kind. Rather, it's what my teachers *embed* each day in their teaching—that's where the connection is made and the difference is felt by the students," Tomlinson comments.

Mural in School Cafeteria Promotes Rachel's Challenge

The lesson here is that a thoughtful blending of different resources combined with the teaching staff's attention to the message they send is sufficient to give rise to a very particular and particularly effective school culture. As an example, this year, Atlantis has accepted Rachel's Challenge.[21] In each classroom, often alongside the class rules, is a "character chain" made out of paper links that are awarded for individual acts

Children at the End of the Year Celebrate the Success of Rachel's Challenge

of kindness and compassion recognized in that class. "The goal," Tomlinson points out, "is to create a chain that goes around the entire school by the end of the year." The picture is rather compelling: individual acts of human goodness combine to surround an institution. It is hard to overestimate what a positive impression that collective act will have both on the students themselves and the school as a whole the day they come together to see the sum total of their good works on display.

How does all this fit together with the six virtues named on the pillars out front? "The pillars form the basis of how the school thinks and speaks about character," Tomlinson answers. "Every year a theme is chosen to *deepen*, or *enrich*, or *rejuvenate* the school's commitment to character. But we couldn't do these yearly themes if the pillars were not in place."

The school adheres to the six pillars because the teachers work together to keep it that way. "We are a team," Tomlinson says plainly. "But we are a team that believes school is about much more than reading, writing, and arithmetic. If you have the stress levels and the accountability responsibilities of today—you better work to put the people piece in place first. When we hire, we look for team players who want to help others and who will thrive in this environment."

And what kind of environment is that?

Tomlinson eagerly replies, "School has to be where your heart sings."

However poetic this may sound, the environment that she describes is remarkably in evidence in the way the teachers interact with one another throughout the day.

The school building is organized into pods of four classrooms with a shared resource room in the middle of each pod that opens from the inside into all four classes. This cluster arrangement allows for just the kind of informal interaction that drives authentic teamwork, but the opportunity to work together is further supported by an institutional commitment to grade-level team planning and shared work products. Grade-level teams have forty minutes of planning time each day created by combining classes for the special activities of PE (two times a week), music, art, and computer/media. Grade-level teams decide how to organize the day, split up instructional responsibilities as needed, and achieve their grade-level goals.

The most remarkable aspect of the team effort at Atlantis is the degree to which it is driven by a child-center focus, which itself is driven by the most unique student needs first. Every April, the faculty participates in a three-day planning retreat to create the whole school instructional schedule for the following year starting with the needs of the exceptional students (ESE) first—as special education is known in Florida—and then building from there until the instructional program for every child in all grades is laid out.[22] The ESE program at Atlantis is, not surprisingly, better structured, better staffed, and better resourced than many, as can be seen, for example, in its highly sophisticated deaf education program.

All deaf students, accompanied by interpreters, and exceptional education students are fully immersed in the regular education program with pull outs as needed to supplement the requirements of their Individual Education Plans (IEPs). With the successful implementation of this inclusion model, Atlantis has been able to maintain its *A* status under the Florida grading system and, more important, achieve adequate yearly progress in all subgroups under No Child Left Behind.

Although Tomlinson and Judson have the instructional expertise to bring a high degree of individuation to the overall program, the larger lesson on display at Atlantis is that every child receives the individual attention of the entire program in the same way only the most exceptional student needs are attended to elsewhere. The school is designed to serve every child exceedingly well, not simply to serve well those whom the system provides with exceptional resources.

But properly understood, this can be done anywhere there is good leadership. Schooling is a complex operation and operational resources can be managed well to achieve positive outcomes. The real story at Atlantis, however, is that the faculty members, under the leadership of the administration, are committed to a definition of a child that is broader, deeper, and fuller than what most expect is part of their portfolio as teachers.

Tomlinson and Judson are not just leading a faculty to differentiate instruction to meet individual student needs; rather, they are leading a faculty who believes, as Judson says, "good character is one of the most important things a child can obtain to become a contributing citizen of our noble country."

This is a lesson we should not be surprised to learn from a school on the space coast where courage, hope, tenacity, and perseverance are the required tools of the trade. Similar to other high-reliability organizations—like the Special Forces, deck crews on aircraft carriers, and trauma center response teams—NASA astronauts and the space program as a whole are recognized for the high level of collaboration that characterizes their work and for the *psychological safety* required for them to operate seamlessly in such demanding circumstances. Atlantis shows that great citizens, not just great students, can be produced by a school that operates like a team in a high-reliability organization. But they, the teachers, need the psychological safety of a high-reliability organization to work this closely together to produce a child who is not just a great student but a trustworthy, respectful, responsible, caring, and fair citizen.

"Real learning occurs when students are able to interact with each other," Judson explains. "The same idea holds true with teachers; yet teachers, by the very nature of their job, are often isolated much of the day in the classroom." Finishing her colleague's observation, almost as if to demonstrate the point, Tomlinson adds, "So the challenge becomes providing support and time for teachers to be able to learn with each other. We do this in our professional learning communities—and this can be life changing for a school." But it takes psychological safety to bring that about.

Speaking to teachers throughout the day is not easy at Atlantis because they are either in their classrooms or working with one another on the work ahead, which is sacrosanct planning time at the school and jealously guarded. But I am fascinated as I watch them work among one another and ask myself what does it take to make an environment in a school safe, not just for children, but for adults?

On the wall, in the school lobby is a poster that flew aboard the shuttlecraft Atlantis on mission STS-117 from June 8th to June 22nd in 2007. Like the classroom rules, but for the whole school, it is signed by more than 700 children. "Pretty cool, huh?" I hear someone ask behind me. The question comes from Candace Jones, a reading coach.

"Amazing," I reply. But then I ask her, what do teachers really learn at this school that makes their work with the children so special. "The teachers here are safe to fail," she replies, "so they try something harder or riskier until they make visible improvements in areas of real consequence."

I am speechless. As President Kennedy said in 1962, we choose to do these things, not because they are easy, but because they are hard.

12

Grayhawk Elementary

Scottsdale, Arizona

School Information	
7525 E. Grayhawk Drive Scottsdale, AZ 85255 Phone: (602) 449–6600	Public 821 students Kindergarten through Grade 6 88% white, 7% Asian, 3% Hispanic, 2% black

Cultural Traits Highlighted	Key Practices Featured
• A strong belief that culture determines outcomes	• Core Knowledge curriculum
• A culture committed to student success	• Student/parent handbook
• A culture of people, principles, and purpose	• The Other 3Rs—citizenship program

As I am admiring one of the dozens of bulletin boards at Grayhawk Elementary, an enormous shadow looms over me cloaking entirely from view what I was reading of the Aztec, Mayan, and Inca cultures. Turning around, I am almost face-to-face with the belt buckle of a modern-day giant and wondering if maybe I was witnessing the rebirth of the Aztec god of war. Looking up, to what feels like three feet above me, I speak briefly with Tom Chambers—the former power forward of the Phoenix Suns, NBA All-Star Game MVP, and television commentator. He's come to school to drop off his son's musical instrument. As Chambers heads down the hall, and the shadow recedes, I go back to reading the bulletin board and reconsider in a new way what I know about the daily passing of Inti, the Inca sun god.

Exterior of Grayhawk Elementary

Grayhawk Elementary is located in Scottsdale, Arizona, a well-to-do suburb of Phoenix known for its well-heeled residents and world-class golf courses. It's the kind of place Tom Chambers might raise his family. But no matter that the school serves families who can generally be described as upper-middle class and up; of the thirty-one elementary schools in the very high-achieving Paradise Valley school district, Grayhawk is the very best. Between 95% and 97% of all students, in all grades, in all subjects are proficient on Arizona's state accountability exams, even if in Paradise Valley one out of five students on average are not proficient on these tests.

Great school cultures are visibly great. Students should be able to see with their own eyes what their school values, what their school teaches, and what their school wants them to learn.

Core Knowledge schools celebrate learning. For this reason, the life of the mind and the love of learning are always on display. Artwork is everywhere: both classic examples of fine art and student imitations of world masterpieces. Classrooms overflow with project posters, dioramas, working models, and historical timelines. The tools of the trade are always in evidence—more like a living museum than anything else—so that the children can experience for themselves how the greatest ideas were first discovered and what those notions look like today: the abacus, slide rule, and calculator; hourglass, pendulum clock, and spring-loaded watch; and dictionaries, encyclopedias, and maps of every kind. But above all else, in the hallways of Core Knowledge schools, there are the bulletin boards—the public displays of those major themes that the Core Knowledge sequence visits year after year so that students of all ages might acquire new knowledge that builds on what they've learned before.

Core Knowledge is at the core of Grayhawk's climate and culture. Core Knowledge is an elementary and middle school program that insists on a solid, specific, shared core curriculum to help children establish strong foundations in all the basic skills across all subject areas. Starting in kindergarten, students learn basic facts in various subjects including, language arts, history, geography, math, science, and the fine arts. Teachers at each grade level are expected to follow the same curriculum to establish a core understanding of each subject and to guarantee a mastery of the principal facts and skills required to participate in each successive grade. The sequence that Core Knowledge specifies was chosen from extensive research into the content and structure of the highest-performing elementary school systems around the world.

Bulletin Boards Throughout the School Celebrate Core
Knowledge

"If you want a layman's definition of Core Knowledge,"
says Don Hiemstra, principal of Grayhawk since its founding thirteen years ago, "it's rich content, rich content, rich
content."

"In this era of testing," Hiemstra continues, "you need
Core Knowledge even to get the humanities *in*. We set high
minimum objectives for *all* kids. Sadly, most schools
define their goals not knowing what *most* kids are really
capable of."

It does not take long to realize that Hiemstra is seriously wor-
ried about the overall quality of schooling today. He asks out
loud, "Is 'no child left behind' because no child is getting ahead?"

Grayhawk was founded in response to the phenomenal
growth in the Paradise Valley school district. Twenty
elementary schools alone have opened in the thirty-one
years Hiemstra has lived there. He successfully opened
another new school before starting Grayhawk, and the

reward for his success was to do it again. But as he describes it, the founding of Grayhawk reveals both what matters to a great school culture and what is required to bring it into being.

"We had a whole year to prepare before the doors opened," Hiemstra explains. "The parents in the area already had a phenomenal school to send their children to, but I invited anyone who would come to meet monthly to dream about opening the school of our dreams." Among the many local citizens who showed up, two did not even have children yet—so engaged was the community in the opportunity offered.

The outcome of these meetings was a statement of parents' ideals converging on three essential ingredients: (1) challenging curriculum, (2) positive communication between home and school, and (3) student pride. Hiemstra quickly landed on the Core Knowledge model as the means to supplying the challenging curriculum. After he took a cadre of teachers to a model visitation school to see it for themselves, they were instantly hooked.

The school opened with 531 students that first year and was so successful it grew to 1,244 by year four. Since then, Pinnacle Peak Elementary School was built to relieve Grayhawk, and Mountain Trail Middle School was opened shortly afterward. Both of these schools, inspired by Grayhawk's success and parent demand for what it has to offer, are themselves strong Core Knowledge schools as well.

"Our vision for the school was so clear in our minds and the teaching staff was so fired up for Core Knowledge that we knew it was going to be a success. But there were a few things those first few years we didn't expect."

Hiemstra goes on to list three unexpected outcomes all related to Core Knowledge's rich content:

- Teachers felt newly empowered to teach.
- Children can retain a massive amount of information.
- Knowledge builds on knowledge—both accelerating student learning and the capacity to learn.

All three of these outcomes are still richly present in the school today. The students are naturally inquisitive, quick in conversation, and endlessly enthusiastic in their desire to learn. As for the teachers, no matter how accomplished, they still exert mammoth effort to bring increased creativity to the classroom, but it is an effort regularly rewarded with new insights, deeper student–teacher relationships, and lasting professional growth. "No doubt about it, you have to be passionate to do this," says Marian Miller, one of the three sixth-grade teachers, "but just look at what they give you in return!" Amid piles of essays and student journals capturing their latest reflections on the literature they are reading and the social history they are studying, you literally cannot get around all the student-made artifacts in the classroom dedicated to the difference between kinetic and potential energy and how energy is conserved in a system.

School Library at Grayhawk Promotes a Vibrant Literary Culture

Great schools always cultivate a literary environment. But this is especially true in Core Knowledge schools where primary sources are venerated and books are the principal means to so much knowledge acquisition. The library is always a special place held in especially high esteem where Core Knowledge is taught.

The library at Grayhawk is a beautifully equipped facility with a high-vaulted ceiling and warm natural lighting that draws you in to its treasures. An enormous number of volumes are flawlessly shelved on low-standing, child-friendly carrels interspersed with carefully crafted and decoratively illustrated display areas highlighting major Core Knowledge themes for the students to explore. A whole section dedicated to the fine arts is exclusively reserved for parents to check out and take home. Upon leaving the library you'll see a prominent sign:

Respect Yourself

Respect Others

Be Responsible

At Grayhawk, these imperatives are known as "The Other 3Rs." In the school's founding, when the community was dreaming of the perfect school, part of the design had to include an antibullying program of some kind, as required by state law. True to the school's plan of being founded on parental ideals, Hiemstra turned to the parents to develop the program. Based on what they say and do at home, they came up with The Other 3Rs, which they also refer to as the school's citizenship program.

"I wanted to build school pride around The Other 3Rs," Hiemstra recounts. "Together they say, 'this is who we are and this is what we value.' Bullying is such a negative concept and citizenship is so central to Core Knowledge; it just seemed to fit."

In the Grayhawk student/parent handbook, which every family must sign to indicate that they have reviewed and will comply with all the policies of the school, an entire page, laid out in print some five times larger than the rest of the handbook, is dedicated to The Other 3Rs. In his letter to the families about the program, Hiemstra writes the following:

> Citizenship is defined as "the character of an individual viewed as a member of society." Good citizenship on school grounds requires that all of us (staff, parents, and students) show respect for the rights of others. Students are expected and required to treat staff, other students, and adults on campus with respect, dignity, and kindness. They are to recognize the value of each individual person and work toward respectful relationships.

With this, the description of the Citizenship Program as it appears in the handbook concludes by saying, "To ensure that children and staff work in a Bully-Free Zone, we need to learn The Other 3Rs."

"It is *the* defining aspect of our school," says Jerry Mogalian, another sixth-grade teacher. "Take a look at the student report card. The academic expectations are on the left—study skills and citizenship are on the right. Without citizenship, you aren't a student at Grayhawk."

Hiemstra makes a similar observation from a different angle, "If a child's citizenship is in order, then you know their grades reflect the very best they can do." With that one sentence, you understand exactly how important The Other 3Rs are to everything that happens at Grayhawk.

For a school largely designed by parents with positive communication between home and school as a basic design principle, it should come as no surprise that the parents are fiercely loyal to the school. What may be unexpected out of so cohesive a community, however, is the degree to which the parents say The Other 3Rs benefit them at home.

Laura Williams sent all three of her boys through Grayhawk, the eldest of whom is now a freshman at Duke University. "What the community wants is not only supported but positively improved here—we're better at home for what takes place at the school," Williams states matter-of-factly. "Kids who might not come from as supportive a background at home are snapped out of it when they come here because they feel like it is a family and everyone tells them to respect themselves, respect others, and be responsible," Another parent of Grayhawk alumni, Peter Rubin, says, "The culture of the 3Rs radiates through this staff. The kids who come out of here are leaders because they are told to respect themselves. Their teachers find out what is good in each of them, feed that, and help it to grow. When the whole staff treats you the same way, you can't help but grow as a result."

In a rather large focus group of current parents, they can barely contain themselves in their description of how important Grayhawk's ideal of citizenship is to driving the school's many other outstanding qualities. "The children are so confident in this environment," one parent says. "They are told to respect others, but their own teachers respect them so much, they risk more and accomplish more." Another parent agrees. "Our kids our risk takers. They learn through their studies; that is part of the project of life—but they are safe to take risks here because of the 3Rs."

Next, the discussion among the parents turns to how well the students speak publicly at Grayhawk because they always have a forum that is open to new ideas and because that forum is so respectful of others. "The children are nurtured and safe here," another parent comments, "because of that, they do what they might never have done elsewhere." Or as Laura Williams summarized it in another conversation, "Unless children are loved, they won't want to perform. But when people who love you are happy with you—you try harder—both for them and for yourself."

For Don Hiemstra, this is the real value of a positive communication channel between home and school: It brings the spirit of home into the school. As his last name would suggest to some, Hiemstra came from a small town in western Michigan. "I believe the local public school needs to create the spirit of the small town and become family," Hiemstra explains. "If you are careful about how people are treated, if you have genuine pride in your school, you can create a positive culture that creates an intrinsic motivation in students. But really, it's like real estate. Instead of 'location,' it's communication, communication, communication."

13

An Achievable Dream

Newport News, Virginia

School Information	
726 16th Street Newport News, VA 23607	Public Prekindergarten through Grade 5 672 students
Phone: (757) 928–6827	Public Magnet Grades 6 through 12 315 students 96% black, 2% Hispanic, 1% white
Cultural Traits Highlighted	**Key Practices Featured**
• A strong belief that culture determines outcomes	• Social, academic, and moral education curriculum • Career curriculum
• A nurturing but demanding culture	• Morning program
• A culture of people, principles, and purpose	• School pledge

Bright-yellow buses pull up alongside the squat, 1970s-issue public school building that once was the Dunbar-Erwin Elementary School. Neatly uniformed students wearing polo shirts tucked squarely into dark navy trousers fall into line. On the back of each of their shirts is an upside-down equilateral triangle with a person pictured at the vertex. The person is labeled YOU. In the middle of the triangle it says, "Make the *Right* Decision." At the base of the triangle, as if off

Logo That Appears on the Back of the Shirt of All Academy Students

in the distance—but clearly within reach of the person depicted—it says, "An Achievable Dream."

As the children walk up the poured concrete stairs on their way to the main entrance, they pass several uniformed active-duty soldiers from the local Army Command at Fort Eustis. "Good morning, Dreamers!" one soldier bellows. A few of the students look up and smile. The others keep walking while trying to shake off their sleep.

Once inside, the single-file line of students is greeted at the entranceway by the school's principal, its executive director, and three other uniformed soldiers. Every child shakes the hand of each person in the receiving line no matter how many guests, corporate executives, or other soldiers may be there that day. The adults make sure the students make eye contact with each of them. Every handshake is joined by an individual greeting of "Good morning!"

Academy Students Shaking Hands With Soldiers at the Start of the Day

SOCIAL, ACADEMIC, AND MORAL EDUCATION

Since its founding in 1992 as an afterschool tennis and tutoring program, the heart and soul of An Achievable Dream has been its unwavering commitment to what it calls a social, academic, and moral education. Both the consistency with which An Achievable Dream always speaks of these three components operating in tandem and the innovation called on to bring them to life are a study in school design.

"Hooah!" a U.S. Army soldier cries out.

"Hooah! Hooah!" several hundred third-, fourth-, and fifth-grade students reply to start the school's morning program. The kindergarten through second grade will arrive later in the morning. The middle and high school students are on another campus a few minutes down the road.

One small third-grade Dreamer walks to the head of the assembly. After the students perform a quick self-check of their uniform, the soldiers throughout the room oversee a more comprehensive inspection of the students' uniforms and overall appearance. Once everyone is squared away, the tiny Dreamer at the head of the room leads the school in the Pledge of Allegiance and the singing of the National Anthem. Fifteen large, white banners hanging on the wall convey the spirit and language of the school's core beliefs.

Schools are first and foremost places of learning. An Achievable Dream's insistence on rigorous academic standards and engaging instructional strategies is no different than what should be expected of every school in the country. The school's explicit teaching, however, that academics must be housed in a social environment that fosters both individual and collective responsibility takes on a new dimension when the school further insists that a moral environment must guide the social and academic components of the program. The students start to recite from the banners on the wall.

"Decisions are up to me!" one tiny little Dreamer calls out.

"Decisions are up to me!" the whole assembly replies in unison.

"Being a success means doing my best!"

"Nothing was ever achieved without enthusiasm!"

"I am somebody!"

An Achievable Dream teaches that unless and until a school community *internalizes* what it values and changes what it wants and desires, no change simply in what it *does* will amount to anything over time. It is essential to spell out the rules of what behavior is expected, but until you institutionalize an environment in which the members of that community are *resolved* to be good citizens of that community, you do not have a community at all, but only a vision of one.

To go further, without a moral code to which the members of the community freely assent to commit themselves, you do not truly have a school either—just a collection of people following a set of rules.

This is the engine that powers An Achievable Dream: academic achievement requires a safe, orderly, and respectful social environment for it to take root. But any genuine social order requires an individual moral commitment to that social order if its aspirations are to be realized.

As the symbol on the back of their shirts indicates, YOU have to make the right decision—if you want to achieve your dreams.

REFORM MISSION AND FOUNDING

The need for low-income, minority children in the Newport News area to be able to achieve their dreams is immense. Across all major violent crimes—murder, rape, robbery, and aggravated assault—Newport News crime rates are roughly twice the national average. More than 80% of these offenses occur in the poorest neighborhoods, most notably the east end near the harbor of Hampton Roads, where the school is located and the area dominated by low-income public housing. Because the experience of depravity is assumed to be a part of nearly every child who comes to An Achievable Dream, all parents have to pledge not just to be positive role models but also to maintain a drug-free and crime-free household.

Local businessman and civic leader, Walter Segaloff founded the initial program literally as a dam to stop children in their earliest years from getting caught in the flow of failure. The idea to couple tennis with afterschool tutoring was intended to match real-world basic skills with a new vision of what any child could achieve in this world.

Perceived as a socially elite sport, it costs very little to get started in tennis, and through it, one can develop important skills of focus, self-discipline, and endurance while learning the manners, rules, and expectations of a game that can be played throughout one's professional life. Within two years, Segaloff had grown the program into a full-time extended-day school for more than 400 third, fourth, and fifth graders and established the relationship with soldiers from Fort Eustis to serve as role models for the children and to help personify the school's culture as a driven and high-achieving environment. With tennis still at the center of the school's identity, An Achievable Dream has been a year-round, extended-day kindergarten through Grade 12 school for more than ten years now delivering on its mission:

> To challenge and motivate all students to exceed their own expectations in academic achievement and social progress and to instill in all children respect for themselves, respect for their adult leaders, and respect for core human values by providing all children with a social, academic, and moral education.

SOCIAL AND MORAL FORMATION

The methods by which An Achievable Dream accomplishes its mission are just as audacious as the mission itself, beginning with the school's pledge and the scope of its social curriculum.

The pledge is a set of eight rhyming couplets, the first two lines of which read, "Today, I'll try to do my best/I will speak green and put street talk to rest." To "speak green" is to speak proper English as it is understood in the world of business where "green" or money is to be made. In other words, the school uses slang to teach its students the absolute necessity for them to rise above the language of the street—while acknowledging that street talk is a reality (and a survival skill) they can only temporarily leave behind while in school. On a much higher note, the pledge concludes with "A Dreamer I am and will always be/For the life of a Dreamer comes from the greatness in me."

Academy Students Line Up in a Hallway

Even if the school's ultimate success (as the pledge indi-cates) hinges on the students making an individual moral assent to the school's mission—An Achievable Dream is not naïve. It understands the very real need for its students to be exposed to new behaviors first before it can expect them to want those behaviors for themselves or appreciate what those behaviors can do for them. For this reason, a whole portion of each day is set aside for the social curriculum.

The social curriculum rotates students through six interre-lated disciplines intended to give them the essential nonacad-emic skills required for them to be successful in the workplace and in civil society. Although it is courageous of the school to say openly that first impressions matter and so assume the obligation of teaching the social norms common to successful and productive citizens, the genius of the program lies in how the curriculum escalates up from proper grammar through the habits of the socially graceful to teach the moral compe-tencies required of the ethically good person. In outline, the six courses might be roughly described as follows:

1. *Speaking green* teaches students to learn the language of success; they learn to desire both proper language and grammar as the linguistic currency of the successful businessman.

2. *Financial know how* builds off this desire for success to expose students to the practical skills of personal finance.

3. *Healthy living* reinforces the school's atmosphere of neatly groomed students and extends that discipline to an understanding of personal hygiene, balanced nutrition, and safety in the home.

4. *Etiquette* taught in a classroom set up as a mock dining room complete with chandelier and formal place settings helps students come to appreciate the language and real utility of social manners.

5. *Peaceful conflict resolution* teaches students through role-playing how to deescalate situations without the violence that is expected on the street and without losing personal status or dignity among their peers.

6. *Ethics,* as the highest expression of the social curriculum, helps students discuss the moral life and learn how to make the right decision with the goal being to make right thinking and good conduct a matter of habit.

Judi Overbey has been teaching and coaching at An Achievable Dream for twelve years (in addition to being the head coach of Northrop Grumman's Apprentice School women's basketball team, which she led two years in a row to the USCCA national championships). She designed and led the morning program earlier in the day. I ask what is the biggest benefit of the morning program. "They feel relaxed afterward," she says. "They feel safe and loved, and we make that solid connection with them that is essential to what we do here." Lee Vreeland, the director of education and student support services, agrees. "Our children come from places that are not happy. You'll find that they are relaxed and want to be here." Catina Bullard-Clark, the school principal, chimes in after listening to her team. "The *relationship* has to come first, so the children know that you care. Only then will you be given the opportunity to make demands on them."

What is the net effect of the morning program and the social rotations on the children? Overbey replies, "They see themselves as people who are going to be successful—as winners. They have no fears, they're driven, and they believe they can do it."

There is no doubt about it; An Achievable Dream is a focused and disciplined environment, but what about the presence of the soldiers and all that screaming in union? Does that really form elementary students to be self-reliant and self-confident? Overbey smiles as if relieved that the question was asked so directly, happy that her work will not be misunderstood. "The students learn to code switch from the language of the street to business language," she explains in the vernacular of the Dreamers. "Well, I have to code switch to give them the structure they require and be more military than is natural to me. But there is an underlying tone of warmth and caring amid the discipline and the structure here. They know they can get whatever they need from one of the adults in this building—and that's where genuine self-reliance begins: in having the confidence to work with others."

A World Apart

It goes without saying that the social and moral formation of the students at An Achievable Dream is all in service to the school's high academic expectations. The school was founded with a strong intention to advance an education reform model that could help close the achievement gap between children in poverty and their more affluent counterparts. In the elementary years, the school is still struggling to close that gap faster, but the school appears to be pursuing a winning strategy by being patient in the early grades and tilling the soil to accept the seed of demanding academic work by focusing first on the social and moral formation of the students. As living proof that this method works, by the middle school years, An Achievable Dream is another world entirely.

A short way down Marshall Avenue, past the small wood-siding houses with the clotheslines out front and the gray Section 8 public developments, you soon come upon the completely remodeled and newly refinished campus of An Achievable Dream's combined middle and high school. The sign outside the front door smartly reads, "No headwear allowed inside the building unless it's a graduation cap." No matter how much this might sound like the uniform standards of the elementary school academy—you have walked onto another planet.

Inside the entranceway, the layout and color palate is pulled straight from the high-end of corporate America. Wood-paneled walls, burnished floors, an HD television tuned quietly to the CNBC finance channel keeps you apprised of your latest investments. A stock-market ticker runs at the bottom of the monitor. You aren't being prepared for success—this is what success looks like. You could be in the receiving room at DuPont Chemical, Bloomberg News, or Berkshire Hathaway. Maybe Google, but there would be a Nerf net somewhere.

Quentin Jackson, a member of the founding staff, was a criminal and social justice major in college, then served abroad in Europe for the U.S. military, and now has returned to the high school at An Achievable Dream as a career counseling administrator. Jackson walks me past a number of the classrooms, each of which is named for a classical virtue or character trait: humility, sincerity, self-reliance, perseverance, patriotism, faith, innovation, and courage. There are thirty-two in all. No matter how restrained the color tones and corporate graphics may be throughout the building, the names of the virtues boldly jump off the walls. Each one is illustrated by a quotation or two and an important number of the rooms feature corporate sponsorships representing that particular entity's support of the school and the role that virtue plays in their success. The Innovation Room, for example, is supported

Sign Outside An American Dream's Combined Middle and
High School Campus

through the generosity of Smithfield Foods. A quotation by
Denis Waitley reads, "You have all the reason in the world to
achieve your grandest dreams. Imagination plus innovation
equals realization."

Jackson summarizes the design quite elegantly: "Everything
I've done well, I've modeled after another adult in my life.
Here we encourage them to model themselves after the best
there are."

After sitting in on a number of classrooms where the high
school and middle school students are busily at work in the
core subject areas, Kelly Alvord, the school's director of special

events, walks me through the broadcast studio, where students get videotaped and receive professional feedback on their interview or presentational skills; the distance learning lab where university-level correspondence courses are taken; and the dining hall, which, to be honest, is more carefully maintained than what the executive trainees at the Marriott Corporation must experience. Alvord notes my surprise. "This is business," she explains. "Dining here is more formal than it is at home, we tell the students. It looks different, and you have to act differently here. This way the students are comfortable when they find themselves in this setting on a job interview someday. The most important interviews take place over a meal."

The explicit angle that An Achievable Dream has pursued, given the deep bench of corporate sponsorship it has amassed and the real need for the students to develop marketable, job-worthy skills, is to morph the social curriculum of the younger years into a "career curriculum" in which the social and behavioral expectations of the school are made more desirable for the greater career opportunities they can help the students realize.

ACHIEVING EXCELLENCE

The completeness of the design is so thorough as to utterly take your breath away. If you are not careful, you can almost forget that just up the road are a couple hundred youngsters whose lives have to be completely transformed before they can be at home in this different environment. At the high school level, there are no uniforms, just a professional dress code. There is no military presence, just a partnership with the local police and sheriff's departments, so a few more positive role models can be on hand. Etiquette is now lived out in the formal dining room, and the students are expected to speak green in person with the corporate executives who come to visit them on campus. The external order and discipline of the elementary school academy, by design, is giving way to an internal moral order and striving for excellence required at the middle and high school.

Richard Coleman, the schools' executive director, puts it this way, "The principles put in place at the academy *expand* when the students come to the high school. Through practice and application they learn both the hard and soft skills they need to be successful in life."

And success is coming their way. After surpassing their citywide peers in mathematics, social studies, science, and English language arts at the middle school level, they soon far exceed the citywide competition and begin to well surpass their state-level peers in the high school exams. One hundred percent of Dreamers taking Algebra II in 2008 passed the Virginia Standards of Learning test while in that same year 96% and 95% of them passed the state geometry and geography exams, respectively. Eighty-four percent of Dreamers who have completed the program are currently enrolled in college, have graduated from college, or are serving in the military.

In considering what An Achievable Dream has accomplished and what lessons it teaches for those who would like to replicate its success, it is important to remember that it is a public magnet school operated in partnership with Newport News public schools and the business community. Sixty-five percent of applicants to the academy or elementary school are drawn from the local attendance zone with the balance of the slots going to those students in the district with the greatest need. By all accounts, the absolutely critical component in this arrangement has been the operating agreement between the school and the district that has allowed An Achievable Dream the flexibility to operate in the best interest of its students. Richard Coleman explains: "The agreement allows us to tailor education infused with the social and moral elements at both schools, even implementing policies and procedures that are not popular with mainstream beliefs about education. These include our early adoption of longer school days, mandatory uniforms, year-round school, and Saturday school many years ago."

Walter Segaloff's leadership has obviously been instrumental in this regard. Even though the state of Virginia has one of the poorest charter school laws in the country and only limited experience with contract schools, Segaloff and his team—powered by the many community interests he has brought on board—have consistently won over the district superintendent and school board members to keep in place what the students enjoy today. Coleman believes this combination of a sound agreement backed by the team's consistent execution has given the school greater latitude to implement techniques that would have been difficult to implement districtwide. "While the school system ensures accountability for academic standards, this agreement has given significant autonomy to An Achievable Dream and is a major factor in it success." Coleman continues by saying, "Working with the school system to provide buses to all students, building maintenance, academic curriculum oversight, and other logistics has allowed An Achievable Dream to focus on the key elements of our school culture and student success."

Although it has not been relevant to An Achievable Dream, school systems that have strong local teacher unions may also need to consider a new kind of partnership or operating agreement with those organizations to develop a school of this kind. Coleman explains it this way, "Ensuring that the teachers' role in the school is not restricted and allowed to adapt throughout the school year is crucial. For An Achievable Dream, our operating agreement dictates that teachers are able to work the longer hours and an occasional Saturday school, for example, with compensation. An agreement with the unions to allow for flexibility and change serving the best interest of the students would be needed."

Down another passage of slick corporate corridors, past the science labs, and past an elegant library also designed to highlight the moral and intellectual virtues key to success in school, you can hear off in the distance the distinct rhythmic popping of tennis balls being hit back and forth. Built into the very middle of the new school's campus is a complete tennis facility. In between classes, one student, focused intently on the wall before him is rhythmically, consistently, pounding a single ball to within fifteen inches of a single mark, some fifteen inches above where a regulation net would stand. A young black man, all alone in Newport News, is working on his game in between classes. It reminds you of the quotation from Arthur Ashe (1995), "You are never really playing an opponent. You are playing yourself, your own highest standards, and when you reach your limits, that is real joy."

14

Benjamin Franklin Classical Charter Public School

Franklin, Massachusetts

School Information	
201 Main Street Franklin, MA 02038 Phone: (508) 541–3434 Fax: (508) 541–5396	Public Charter 394 students Kindergarten through Grade 6 89% white, 8% Asian, 1% black, 1% Hispanic
Cultural Traits Highlighted	**Key Practices Featured**

• A strong belief that culture determines outcomes	• Four cardinal virtues:
	   (1) justice
	   (2) temperance
	   (3) fortitude
	   (4) prudence
	
	• Student statement
	• Forest of Virtue

• A culture committed to student success	• Parent and teacher resource guides
• A culture of people, principles, and purpose	• Faculty input team

Founded in 1995, Benjamin Franklin Classical Charter Public School (BFCCPS) is one of the oldest charter schools in the country. A charter school is a public school freed from many of the bureaucratic rules and regulations that constrain other public schools in exchange for greater accountability for results. Benjamin Franklin shares both this attribute as a charter school and its commitment to classical education with Veritas Academy in Phoenix. Like P.S. 124 and Grayhawk Elementary, it is also a Core Knowledge school. Then, of all the great school cultures in the country that could have been featured here to tell us a new story, what does BFCCPS teach us?

BFCCPS teaches us how to survive—how school cultures must adapt—and how a community must continue to choose the explicit character formation of its children if it wants to harness that character to drive achievement.

ACADEMIC EXCELLENCE

BFCCPS is one of the highest performing charter schools in the state of Massachusetts, which has one of the better charter school laws in the country. People who are critical of the law fault it for its cap on the number of charters in the state while others argue that this cap has helped the state maintain a high level of quality. In the midst of this debate, BFCCPS is still a standout by any means.

On the Massachusetts state assessment tests, the third grade ranked tenth in reading out of the 1,013 schools in the state that have a third grade. Similarly, the sixth grade ranked fourteenth out of 565 in English while the eighth grade ranked first of 462 in science.[23] At the same time, 88% of BFCCPS students who took the National Latin exam scored above 75% while 87% of them scored above 75% on Le Grand Concourse, which the sixth through eighth graders take to determine their proficiency in French language arts.

Ironically, however, according to some, this heavy-duty focus on testing has strained the school internally and pulled it off its strong foundations. It may also be that this internal debate over what the school is trying to achieve is precisely what the school needs to remain strong. If the lessons taught in this book are correct, then it is in how the school culture responds to this challenge that its future will be determined.

From its original charter, BFCCPS was founded on four pillars. The mission of BFCCPS is "to assist parents in the role as *primary educators* of their children by providing the children with a *classical academic education* coupled with sound *character development* and opportunities for *community service*." These four pillars are deep concepts carefully articulated in the school's founding documents and artfully communicated to parents, students, and teachers over the years. As an example of this, the school has the following to say on what it means for a parent to be a child's primary educator:

A child is first taught by his or her parents and continues to be profoundly influenced by them throughout life. As an expression of the deep love they have for their children, parents assume the ultimate responsibility of ensuring their children receive the education they will need to succeed in tomorrow's world. Parents choose their children's schools carefully and follow their studies closely, acting as true partners with teachers in all that they do.

What is more, the role of the parent in partnership with the school is explicitly stated as supporting the other pillars. In answering the question, how can parents best be involved in their child's education? the school replies, "Parents can support the classroom teaching of their children by making curricular connections at home, modeling virtue, and engaging in community service activities."

These are not words taken lightly. This is solemn counsel from a school that reveres the moral authority of the parent in the home while also understanding clearly its own moral obligation to advise its parents well and instruct them in those duties that will best serve their children and their children's efforts in school.

This is precisely the kind of communication that great school cultures are made of. What effect does it have on the community?

"It creates some of the most well-rounded students I have ever worked with," say Joe Perna, the director of school operations and student activities. "The founders had the vision that the common language of the pillars would allow character to inform content at every turn." And this is exactly what the school has always proudly stood for.

True to its classical origins and modeled on the great academies of the past, BFCCPS clearly understands that the mission of education is to help students become both learned and good. As its framework for explicitly teaching to character, the school has always used the four cardinal virtues of (1) justice, (2) temperance, (3) fortitude, and (4) prudence and then filled these out by speaking in class to the many related virtues and character traits that follow them. Prudence leads to discussions of honesty and integrity, for example, while fortitude leads to the related virtues of courage, sacrifice, and perseverance. Stories and heroes exemplifying each of these virtues abound. And the discussing of these stories, in turn, can give rise to the deepest and most exciting explorations of the human condition.

The expectation for all teachers at BFCCPS is that this kind of conversation will take place in many forms throughout the day, whether by discussing these themes in social studies and language arts, by debating the moral actions of characters they read about, or through students journaling their personal reflections in diaries maintained to capture the development and formation of their interior life. If this sounds quaint or overly idealistic in any way, stop yourself.

In all American letters, there is perhaps no other single personality so associated with this activity of privately moralizing (and then trying to make the most of it for public benefit) than Benjamin Franklin himself. It goes without saying that schools that have an easy touchstone of this kind, like the school's namesake, can more easily work these activities into their daily routines and so fortify the cultural fabric of their school. The question at BFCCPS in recent years, faced with the increasing demands of so much state testing and the accountability requirements to satisfy its charter, was how was the school to work these noble but "nonessential" exercises into its regular routine.

According to some accounts, the school began to drift from its founding and started to lose some of the character of its culture. A number of the founding board members left. A number of the key faculty members left. The school began to change.

Charter schools are unlike local public schools in that they are governed by volunteer school boards. To hold a charter school together, a charter school board must get itself together first and learn to hold a school's administration accountable for the mission and vision stated in the school's charter. This is the great strength of charter schools—they first must say what they aim to do, and then they must do what they say, or they can be closed for failing to deliver on their essential promise.

This direct form of accountability that keeps charter schools true to their mission is a mechanism that can greatly benefit any school drifting away from its founding ideals. As the story of BFCCPS shows, a vigilant focus on mission helps a school culture stay close to what it most holds dear and to correct course if ever it begins to veer from its intended path.

Kevin O'Malley came to BFCCPS as its new head of school three years ago. A traditional schoolman but a former district superintendent, O'Malley looked on paper like the kind of guy who would run BFCCPS by the numbers and make sure it primarily complied with all the bureaucratic requirements with only a secondary concern for the unique qualities of its charter and all that implied.

Luckily, this turned out to be untrue. An old-fashioned Irish-Catholic himself, there was something poetic about him coming to run a school in a predominantly Irish-Catholic community, located in an abandoned 1950s-style Catholic parish school building that has to be evacuated every day by 3:45 for the largest religious education program in the country. He understood what the community needed—and he worked to give it to them.

"The school board serves as the Supreme Court to interpret the founding documents," he comments wryly while getting his point across perfectly: charter school boards, properly understood, need to enforce both the spirit and the letter of the charters entrusted to their care. "The board also has a mission committee and has worked well with a new faculty input team to figure out what in the school needs attending to." However much it may sound as if he's simply taking orders from the board, O'Malley is putting the pieces in place to refocus the school on its founding and to capitalize on its most essential qualities. At the recommendation of the faculty input team, for example, the student statement that was so dear to the school at its founding is now posted throughout the school as just one visible sign of the school's public return to its roots.

"At the board level, we appreciate what makes this school special," says board president Lori Clements. "Now we're measuring performance against our mission looking for opportunities to improve. For one, that means parents as primary educators and, two, our teachers' command of our character education mission."

As all good leaders do, O'Malley has already put his succession plan in place and appointed a new assistant head of school. This gives him more time to spend cultivating the environment and motivating the culture to be focused first on the needs of children—not simply on the need for children to produce a score on a test. In response to the board's direction to redirect teacher training back on to the character education mission, Joe Perna and his team have created new parent and teacher resource guides aligned so that, as the primary educators, parents can reinforce the character formation they can now expect to see more regularly in the classroom.

"People ask what does it mean to teach the whole child?" O'Malley says wistfully. "For one, it means we're not just educating 'the math piece' of the child." And as perhaps only a jovial Irishman can say so directly without fear of insult, he continues, "And two, it means we're educating the whole child." To improve a school, you have to educate more of what's in it, and more than anything, schools are filled with children—the whole of whom need our undivided attention, every day.

While O'Malley and I are talking, streams of little children come into his office to have him personally sign the "leaves of virtue" that they received earlier that morning at the kindergarten assembly. He speaks with and compliments each child one by one on his or her accomplishment, like a mayor of a small town, giving each child his undivided attention while personally reinforcing what the school values most. Once the leaves are signed—leaves that were individually awarded by their teachers for specific habits of prudence, temperance, fortitude, and justice—they will go into the Forest of Virtue where, on display, they will grow, presumably, alongside all the other good acts recently celebrated by the school.

SECTION III

Response

15

How Communities Can Help Form Great School Cultures

This book was written to encourage school leaders and teachers to reconsider how they might change their daily practice. School cultures do not happen by accident. Instead, they are the intended result of much thought and hard work. In the absence of a focused effort to shape and give life to a very particular school culture, a culture of some kind will emerge, but unless it is *purposefully formed*, it will not be a culture that you can *work* with—and it will not necessarily be a culture that is working for you or your students.

But this book was also written for parents, school advocates, and other civic leaders so they might know what to look for in a great school. Although very few people recently have seriously thought to ask the question, "What is a school for?" this book presumes to provide the initial outline of an answer.

By their very design, schools can bring about more of the hardworking, good, and noble student-citizens we need to lead our country prosperously into the future. But schools also need to be designed and maintained in a very certain way to produce this great result with any sort of regularity.

Approximately 90% of all children in America go to public schools. The manner in which state and local laws are written has a spectacular influence on the kind and quality of the schools our children go to. The manner in which school districts are structured and the means by which district priorities are identified also has a tremendous influence on what school communities believe is really important and worth their greatest time and attention. It has been an explicit goal of this book to show that school communities need to focus greater time and attention on the school cultures they create so that our children might receive the education they truly deserve—an education in which not only skills are mastered but children also learn who they are as people and how they can best contribute to their happiness and to the happiness of others.

The stories of the schools profiled here reveal how an intentional school culture can positively inform the lives of children and instill in them a whole array of good habits of lasting consequence. But it must not be forgotten that these schools are not the norm.

Although almost every teacher in America is aware of the moral dimension to their work, the current political, legal, and regulatory environment in which most schools operate is not designed to encourage school cultures that intentionally produce students of strong moral character. This is a fact. And it is a fact that needs to be overcome.

It is not that we, the American people, no longer desire that our schools function as a positive social institution; rather, it is simply that for some time now, our educational system has not expected the depth and range of positive social outcomes—like those produced by the schools documented here—to be a primary by-product of all American schooling. Although the schools presented in these pages demonstrate that it can be done (and provide some insight into how other schools might learn from their experience), it is just as important to recognize the many barriers that prevent even the most well-intended students, parents, teachers, administrators, and school district officials from advocating for more great schools of this kind.

Who teaches, what they teach, and the environment they teach in are all critical to the formation and maintenance of the outstanding school cultures we celebrate in this book. However, improving teacher quality, enriching curricular content, and increasing school-level autonomy—all keys to creating great school cultures—are not the key concerns of most school districts today. Whether this mandate comes from the voters, school district officials, or educators themselves is, for the moment, immaterial.

Why?

Because the school system as a whole in the United States of America is simply not designed to recommend the inputs, monitor the process, or reward the appropriate outcomes to encourage the formation of more schools like those presented here.

Inspired by the lessons learned from these twelve schools, however, interested communities can focus on five areas of opportunity to increase the number of school cultures that intentionally produce students of strong moral character. By focusing on these five opportunities, we can work together to better align the *people* and *principles* at the heart of our nation's school system around one *purpose*—inviting more great school cultures of this kind. The five opportunities are as follows:

1. **Certification**—teacher certification focuses on the wrong criteria and excludes many quality candidates from the teaching profession.
   o This is perhaps most obviously seen in the number of schools featured here that require their teachers to

have an extraordinary command of rigorous curricular content and subject area expertise. The ability to teach demanding content is not a basic expectation of most teacher certification regimes, and what is required to become a certified teacher often limits the opportunity for that teaching candidate to become a subject-area expert.

o As an example, perhaps the single greatest threat to Veritas Academy and the expansion of the Great Hearts school system is teacher certification. The very people Veritas needs to teach its great books program—graduates from some of the most elite liberal arts colleges in the country—are the same people who do not meet typical teacher certification requirements and so are forced away from the school or have to comply with additional bureaucratic hurdles to serve as a teacher there.

o P.S. 124, Grayhawk, and Benjamin Franklin are all Core Knowledge schools. Like Veritas, they too require that their teachers plumb deep academic depths every day at school. It is not the goal of teacher certification, however, to ensure that teachers are capable of delivering this kind of rich instructional experience borne of personal instructional expertise.

2. **Professionalism**—the typical hiring, firing, and career management of teachers does not encourage the building of teaching teams essential to great school cultures.

o Every single academic team interviewed for this book, whether profiled here or not, mentioned the extraordinary professionalism of their colleagues as a key driver of their satisfaction in the job.

o Great school cultures are driven by individuals who are themselves driven by a personal desire to achieve, in concert with others, something great in their work. Bringing people of this mind-set into a school together (and keeping people who do not share this mind-set out of a school) is a key task of school leadership that is often thwarted by flawed personnel policies or more powerful political forces.

o The personal quotations cited in this book from the teachers at Hinsdale Central, Arlington Traditional, HOPE Prima, and Providence St. Mel give us a first taste of what strong teaching teams look like and what kind of freedoms they require not just to serve one another but also our children, in the very best way they can.

3. **Local Autonomy**—school district mandates are often hostile to local autonomy and the formation of individual school cultures of unique identity.

o Ten out of the twelve schools profiled here are public schools. All twelve of the schools featured in this book, however, are extraordinary for their individual character, local autonomy, and their basic insistence that their school-level vision guide their daily action. The freedom of choice to lead unique school cultures of this kind is not, however, a freedom given to most school leaders or welcomed when school leaders try to take this freedom for themselves.

o Public charters and public magnets are given freedoms that many local public schools do not enjoy. We need to encourage the expansion of more magnets and charters. But Hinsdale Central, Harvest Park, Grayhawk, Atlantis, and the very unique story of An Achievable Dream show that local communities can do much more to get exactly the kind of schools they want serving their children.

4. **Standards**—character education norms and social/emotional standards operate at the wrong level to positively impact the formation of good school cultures.

o The stories featured here are simple stories of great schools doing great things at the local level. It is at the local level that great stories are made because it is at the local level that individual children's lives are impacted and positively formed by the lives of others.

o Neither federal nor state mandates promoting various kinds of "character education" will invite more great schools of the kind profiled here. Rather, our concern for standards should be with *academic* standards that demand a certain level of education that simply demands more of everyone.

5. **Curriculum**—curricular content is rarely designed to encourage individual reflection and typically is too thin to invite the deep moral formation of students.

o This is related to but different from the first opportunity regarding teacher certification. This opportunity has more to do with *what* is taught and *how* that teaching is performed than who does the teaching and how they are determined to be qualified to teach. What matters here is that students are stretched and stretched to ask the greatest things of themselves and one another.

o As we have seen, great school cultures are both nurturing and demanding. For schools to be both intellectually nurturing and intellectually demanding, they must inspire students—at age appropriate levels—to engage life's deepest questions. Without inviting matters of religion into the public square, it is the student engagement of philosophically difficult questions that most easily invites the formation of a moral society in school.

o Similarly, if schools are to be morally or socially nurturing and morally or socially demanding, they must require students to give more of themselves individually and expect more of their friends in return. Cotswold's emphasis on daily student reflection in their day books, the Humane Letters seminar at

Veritas, the culture of clubs and community service at Hinsdale, and the love of learning and the commitment to service encouraged at every school celebrated here shows how much more we can get if the curriculum expects that much more of our children and their teachers.

Schooling is a richer, deeper, and more exciting enterprise than what the current system is designed to deliver or what the profession as a whole is instructed to produce. By following the lead of the examples highlighted in *On Purpose*, we have a new opportunity to reignite the moral imagination and remind others what great schools look like. Inspired by these examples, it is now our job to lead a new generation of children through schools that will form them well—form them as people of strong moral character—ready, willing, and able to inherit the future guided by the strong lead of the true, the good, and the beautiful.

Endnotes

1. It was Flip Flippen who first encouraged me to look for *nurturing* and *demanding* qualities that were held in tension in high-performing schools. The observation is a potent one. For more information on the research studies that his group has performed to demonstrate the need for balance across a certain number of specific behavioral indexes, see http://www.flippengroup.com.

2. As we look at individual schools, it becomes very important to understand how the learned behavior (that is generally considered to be a part of a school's tradition) becomes internalized to motivate the lives of its students and helps determine their moral actions and the formation of their personal character.

3. Trinity Schools, established in 1981, is dedicated to "the discovery of truth, the creation of beauty, and the practice of goodness." Today, there are three Trinity School campuses: Trinity School at Greenlawn in South Bend, Indiana; Trinity School at Meadow View in Falls Church, Virginia; and Trinity School at River Ridge in Eagan, Minnesota.

4. National Organization of Women's charter document was written by Betty Friedan, author of *The Feminine Mystique*.

5. *Spotless Rose: Hymns to the Virgin Mary* was the winner of the 2008 Grammy award for Best Small Ensemble Performance.

6. Hinsdale was recently listed as the thirty-second richest zip code in the United States. See http://wealth.mongabay.com/tables/100_income_zip_codes-10000.html.

7. Hinsdale Township High School District 86's two schools, (1) Hinsdale Central and (2) Hinsdale South, serve the seven western suburban communities of (1) Oak Brook, (2) Burr Ridge, (3) Clarendon Hills, (4) Hinsdale, (5) Darien, (6) Willowbrook, and portions of (7) Westmont. The district is 17 miles due west of Chicago's loop.

8. Each year, there are around fifty-five adults on each of three collaborative teams: (1) curriculum, (2) student life (which has sixty to eighty student members), and (3) community connections. A teacher-leader heads each team, and Bylsma oversees the work from a schoolwide perspective. Each team functions as its own entity, but they share minutes with one another, collaborate on events, and utilize members for focus groups and the like.

9. It should not go unnoticed how student achievement, as measured by ACT scores and state-mandated testing, has improved significantly since Hinsdale's deliberate effort to reform its school culture. In 2001, juniors scored an average composite ACT score of 24.5. By 2009, juniors scored an average ACT of 26.4 even though nearly 243 more students were added to that grade level over that period. While ACT predicts expected growth of points from the EXPLORE test in eighth grade to the ACT in eleventh grade, Hinsdale students now average 8.2 points of growth. In 2009, 885 students took 1,890 AP exams with 90% earning a 3, 4, or 5 compared to only 435 students who took 769 exams with an 80% passing rate in 2001. Today, 99% of Hinsdale students are college bound with the vast majority going to four-year private institutions.

10. As but one example, middle school students attending JHS 226 up the street are not fairing so well. According to the New York State School Report Card Accountability and Overview report for 2008–2009, only 66% of students in seventh grade scored at or above Level 3 (meeting learning standards) in English language arts and only 57% of eighth graders.

11. This according to Linda Bevilacqua, president of the Core Knowledge Foundation, and E. D. Hirsch, Jr., the founder of the Core Knowledge program. Since February 23, 2006, P.S. 124 has been recognized by the Foundation as a national visitation site and is only one of two schools in the entire state of New York that has earned that distinction.

12. *Core Virtues* is a literature-based character education program for children written by Mary Beth Klee. According to the publisher, "The *Core Virtues* program is a practical, nonsectarian approach to character education on a kindergarten through sixth-grade level that involves approximately twenty minutes per day of reading and discussion. Its goals are the cultivation of character through such virtues as respect, courage, diligence, patience, responsibility, compassion, perseverance, faithfulness, and more."

13. It is important to note that since the New York City Department of Education developed the Empowerment Organization those that have joined it, as P.S. 124 has, are afforded greater freedoms in running their schools. They have greater freedom with their budget allocation, how they spend their money, their program development, and their hiring. Although the school is held to a higher standard of accountability, it allows schools like P.S. 124 that are "run like a charter school" the ability to grow as they see fit while supporting their creativity.

14. The Virginia Preschool Initiative distributes state funds to schools and community-based organizations to provide quality preschool programs for at-risk four-year-olds unserved by Head Start.

15. For children who read chapter books, every twenty-five pages is considered a book for the purposes of the summer reading challenge.

16. The program has grown from 337 students (FTE) at seven schools in 1990–1991 to 20,328 students (FTE) at 111 schools in 2009–2010. Enrollment is capped by statute at 22,500 students. See http://www.schoolchoicewi.org/k12/detail.cfm?id=4.

17. To learn more about the No Excuses movement see Paul Tough's article in the *New York Times* magazine, "What It Takes to Make a Student" (http://query.nytimes.com/gst/fullpage.html?res=9505E3D7153EF935A15752C1A9609C8B63&sec=&spon=&pagewanted=10) and Jay Mathews article *Naming Our Best Schools* (http://www.washingtonpost.com/wp-dyn/content/article/2008/09/12/AR2008091200631.html).

18. The No Child Left Behind Act of 2001, Sec. 1111 (b)(F), requires that "each state shall establish a timeline for adequate yearly progress. The timeline shall ensure that not later than 12 years after the 2001–2002 school year, all students in each group described in subparagraph (C)(v) will meet or exceed the State's standards." These timelines are developed by state education agencies working under guidance from the federal government. State mandated AYP objectives apply to all students in the tested grades and to subgroups of sufficient size. The subgroups include five major ethnic groups, students with disabilities, English language learners, and economically disadvantaged students.

19. The stated aim of all IB programs is "to develop internationally minded people who, recognizing their common humanity and shared guardianship of the planet, help to create a better and more peaceful world." To this end, the IB learner profile encourages

the growth and development of ten basic traits in all IB students: communicator, risk-taker, knowledgeable, open-minded, reflective, principled, balanced, inquirer, caring, thinker. See *IB Learner Profile Booklet*, published November 2008 by International Baccalaureate Organization, http://www.ibo.org.

20. Challenger 7 is not named for the spacecraft itself but for the seven crew members who died in the second minute of the orbiter's tenth mission on January 28, 1986.

21. Rachel Scott was the first person killed at Columbine High School on April 20, 1999. Rachel's Challenge is an organization founded in her memory "to inspire, equip and empower every person to create a permanent positive culture change in their school, business and community by starting a chain reaction of kindness and compassion." See http://www.rachelschallenge.org.

22. An exceptional student as defined in Rules 6A-6.03011 through 6A-6.03031, FAC, means any child or youth who requires special instruction or related services and is enrolled in or eligible for enrollment in the public schools of a district. This includes all needs identified within IDEIA , the federal government's special education law, but not limited to autism spectrum disorder, deaf/hard-of-hearing, dual-sensory impaired, emotional/behavioral disorders, gifted, homebound or hospitalized, intellectual disabilities, occupational therapy, physical therapy, physically impaired, specific learning disabilities, speech and language impaired, and visually impaired.

23. Overall placement ranks are arrived at by combining the percentage of students who were either advanced or proficient on the Massachusetts state assessment tests and comparing that number for each subject and grade with schools across the state.

References
and Further
Readings

Abbott, J. (1995). Children need communities. *Educational Leadership, 52*(8), 8–10.

Arlington Academy of Hope. (2010). *Our story.* Retrieved August 31, 2010, from http://aahuganda.org/about-us/our-story

Arthur, J. (2003). *Education with character: The moral economy of schooling.* London: Routledge.

Arthur, J., & Godfrey, R. (2005). *Statistical survey of the attainment and achievement of pupils in Church of England schools.* Canterbury, UK: National Institute for Christian Education Research.

Arthur, J., & Revell, L. (2008). *Character formation in schools and the education of teachers.* Canterbury, UK: National Institute for Christian Education Research.

Ashe, A., & McKnab, A. (1995). *Arthur Ashe on tennis: Strokes, strategy, traditions, players, psychology and wisdom.* New York: Knopf, Inc.

Bellah, R. (2007). *Habits of the heart: Individualism and commitment in American life.* Berkeley: University of California Press.

The Benjamin Franklin Classical Charter Public School. (n.d.). *About us.* Retrieved September 1, 2010, from http://www.bfccps.org/main/AboutUs/Mission.asp

The Benjamin Franklin Classical Charter Public School. (n.d.). *Parents as primary educators.* Retrieved September 1, 2010, from http://www.bfccps.org/main/ParentsAsPrimaryEducators/Default.asp

Bennett, W. J. (1988). *Our children and our country: Improving America's schools and affirming the common culture.* New York: Simon and Schuster.

Bennett, W. J. (1993). *The index of leading cultural indicators.* Washington, DC: The Heritage Foundation.

Berkowitz, M. W. (1995). *The education of the complete moral person.* Aberdeen, Scotland: Gordon Cook Foundation.

Berreth, D., & Scherer, M. (1993). On transmitting values: A conversation with Amitai Etzioni. *Educational Leadership, 51*(3), 12–15.

Brooks, B. D., & Kann, M. E. (1993). What makes character education programs work? *Educational Leadership, 51*(3), 19–21.

Carter, S. C. (2000). *No excuses: Lessons from 21 high-performing, high-poverty schools.* Washington, DC: The Heritage Foundation.

Charlotte Chamber of Commerce. (2009). *Population estimates 2009.* Retrieve August 31, 2010, from http://www.charlottechamber.com/demo-ecoprofile/population-estimates-2009

Coles, R. (1996, March). The disparity between intellect and character. *Olivet Notes, 1*(2), 1–4.

Coles, R. (1997). *The moral intelligence of children: How to raise a moral child.* New York: Random House.

Colson, C. (1995). *Reviving the virtues: A 10-part series: Break point.* Washington, DC: Prison Fellowship Ministries.

Colson, C. (1996). *Cultivating character in the classroom: A 9-part series: Break point.* Washington, DC: Prison Fellowship Ministries.

Delattre, E. J. (1992). Diversity, ethics and education in America. *Moral Education Journal,* pp. 70–82.

Dryfoos, J. G. (1994). *Full-service schools: A revolution in health and social services for children, youth, and families.* San Francisco: Jossey-Bass.

Etzioni, A. (1994). *Points of discussion for the White House conference on Character Building.* Washington, DC: The Communitarian Network.

Etzioni, A. (1995, November 13). The politics of morality. *The Wall Street Journal.*

Etzioni, A. (1996, May 29). In character education virtue should be seen, not just heard. *Education Week,* p. 40.

Gauld, J. W. (1993). *Character first: The Hyde School difference.* San Francisco: Institute for Contemporary Studies Press.

Goldberg, M. F. (1995). Portraits of educators: Reflections on 18 high achievers. *Educational Leadership, 52*(8), 72–76.

Goleman, D. (1995). *Emotional intelligence.* New York: Bantam Books.

Haynes, C. C. (1995). Taking religious liberty seriously in school. *The School Administrator, 8*(52), 44.

Heath, D. H. (1994). *Schools of hope: Developing mind and character in today's youth.* San Francisco: Jossey-Bass.

Hunter, J. D. (2001). *The death of character: On the moral education of America's children.* New York: Basic Books.

Jensen, L., & Passey, H. (1993). Moral education curricula in the public schools. *Religion & Public Education, 27*(1), 27–35.

The Josephson Institute. (2010). *Character Counts!* Retrieved October 4, 2010, from http://charactercounts.org/overview/members .php

Kennedy, J. F. (1962, September 12). Address at Rice University on the Nation's Space Effort. Houston, TX.

Kennedy, J. F. (1961, May 25). Special Message to the Congress on Urgent National Needs. Washington, DC.

Lickona, T. (1992). *Educating for character: How our schools can teach respect and responsibility.* New York: Bantam Books.

Lickona, T. (1993). The return of character education. *Educational Leadership, 51*(3), 6–11.

Lickona, T. (1998). A more complex analysis is needed. *Phi Delta Kappan, 79*(6), 449–454.

Lickona, T. (2004). *Character matters: How to help our children develop good judgment, integrity, and other essential virtues.* New York: Touchstone.

Marzano, R. J. (2003). *What works in schools: Translating research into action* (pp. 17–21). Alexandria, VA: ASCD.

MDNH. (2010). *Pleasanton City, California statistics and demographics (US Census 2000).* Retrieved August 31, 2010, from http:// pleasanton.areaconnect.com/statistics.htm

New York State Education Department. (2009). Statewide accountability. In *The New York state report card: Accountability and overview report 2008–09* (p. 10). Albany, NY: Author.

Ravitch, D. (1990). Multiculturalism: E pluribus plures. *The American Scholar, 59*(3), 337–354.

Rehberg, C. D. (1994). *Fundamentals of leadership and character development.* Colorado Springs, CO: United States Air Force Academy, Center for Character Development.

Rest, J. R. (1982). *Components of ethical decision making and behavior: A psychologist looks at the teaching of ethics.* Briarcliff Manor, NY: The Hastings Center.

Roberts, R. (1993). Tough love for kids at risk. *Educational Leadership, 51*(3), 81–82.

Ruenzel, D. (1997, February 5). AVID learners. *Education Week,* pp. 28–33.

Ryan, K. (1993). Mining the values in the curriculum. *Educational Leadership, 51*(3), 16–18.

Ryan, K. (1995). The ten commandments of character education. *The School Administrator, 8*(52), 18–19.

Ryan, K., & Bohlin, K. (2003). *Building character in schools: Practical ways to bring moral instruction to life.* San Francisco: Jossey-Bass.

Ryan, K., & Lickona, T. (Eds.). (1992). *Character development in schools and beyond* (2nd ed., pp. 305–340). Washington DC: The Council for Research in Values and Philosophy.

Sanders, W. L., & Rivers, J. C. (1996). *Cumulative and residual effects of teachers on future student academic achievement*. Knoxville: University of Tennessee Value-Added Research and Assessment Center.

Scoggin, D. (2008). Classical revolution. *Great Hearts: Classical Education, Revolutionary Schools, 1*, 22.

Sergiovanni, T. J. (1995). Small schools, great expectations. *Educational Leadership, 53*(3), 48–52.

Sommers, C. H. (1991). Teaching the virtues. *Imprimis, 20*(11), 1–5.

Sternberg, R. (1990). Practical intelligence for success in school. *Education Leadership, 48*(1), 35–39.

Sternberg, R. (2001). Why schools should teach for wisdom. *Educational Psychologist, 36*(4), 227–245.

Tjart, D., & Boersma, F. J. (1978). A comparative study of religious values of Christian and public school eighth graders. *Journal of Psychology and Theology, 6*(2), 132–140.

Townley, A. (1995). Changing school culture. *Educational Leadership, 52*(8), 80.

U.S. Census Bureau. (2000). *Fact sheet*. Available at http://factfinder.census.gov/servlet/DatasetMainPageServlet?_lang=en

USAF Center for Character Development. (1994). *United States Air Force Academy character development manual*. Colorado Springs, CO: United States Air Force Academy.

Vincent, P. F. (1995). *Developing character in students*. Chapel Hill, NC: New View.

Vincent, P. F. (2003). *Promising practices in character education: 12 success stories from around the country*. Chapel Hill, NC: Character Development Group.

Wynne, E. A., & Ryan, K. (1993). *Reclaiming our schools: A handbook on teaching character, academics, and discipline*. New York: Merrill.

Index

Page references following (figure) indicate an illustrated figure.

CORWIN

A SAGE Company

The Corwin logo—a raven striding across an open book—represents the union of courage and learning. Corwin is committed to improving education for all learners by publishing books and other professional development resources for those serving the field of PreK–12 education. By providing practical, hands-on materials, Corwin continues to carry out the promise of its motto: **"Helping Educators Do Their Work Better."**

Center for Education Reform

The Center for Education Reform drives the creation of better educational opportunities for all children by leading parents, policymakers, and the media in boldly advocating for school choice, advancing the charter school movement, and challenging the education establishment.